POCKET
FANTASY ART

CW00816002

POCKET
FANTASY ART

THE **VERY BEST** IN CONTEMPORARY FANTASY ART & ILLUSTRATION

General Editor **MARTIN MCKENNA**
Foreword by **BORIS VALLEJO**

I L E X

POCKET FANTASY ART NOW

First published in the UK in 2010 by
I L E X
210 High Street
Lewes
East Sussex BN7 2NS
www.ilex-press.com

Copyright © 2010 The Ilex Press Limited

Publisher: Alastair Campbell
Creative Director: Peter Bridgewater
Managing Editor: Nick Jones
Editors: Martha Evatt & Ellie Wilson
Commissioning Editor: Tim Pilcher
Art Director: Julie Weir
Designer: Simon Goggin

British Library Cataloguing-in-Publication Data
A catalogue record for this book is available from
the British Library.

ISBN : 978-1-905814-99-2

10 9 8 7 6 5 4 3 2 1

Printed and bound in China
Colour Origination by Ivy Reprographics

Contents

Foreword

Reality is stranger than fiction, or so we are told. Present technology seems to confirm that statement. The arrival of personal computers has revolutionized the way we do most things in our daily lives, including art. It was not too long ago that Chesley Bonestell amazed the world with hyper-realistic renditions in oil of other worlds' landscapes, and today we have the luxury of seeing this in actual photographs.

The job of a fantasy artist is to even out the odds and make fiction stranger than reality. Years ago, during the first third of the 20th century, publications known as pulps featured fantasy short stories. Accompanied by somewhat garish illustrations, they often showed an artist's vision of alien inhabitants on other planets. For some reason, all of them were very anxious to invade our Earth; it was the infancy of this artistic genre. The artists worked for low pay, and always under the pressure of tough deadlines. The pulps came to an end in the early part of the 1950s, but not before having earned large legions of fans. Although paperback books have been around since the 19th century, the '50s saw the start of higher quality art on the covers of these mass-market publications. The following decade was to be crucial in establishing the quality of an art form that was now achieving maturity.

In order to create a good illustration, an artist must have a number of attributes: training, good imagination, and good narrative, among other things. In order to create a good fantasy illustration, the artist has to also be capable of pulling ideas out of thin air, since often they have to paint things that do not exist. To do this, the artist has to refer to their mental knowledge of things that *do* exist, and be able to modify them to be both strangely different and believable; this is what will make the finished illustration successful.

The 21st century is here.
Is reality stranger than fiction?
Is fiction stranger than reality?
You hold this book in your hands—
you are the judge.

Boris Vallejo, 2007

Introduction

Bringing this book to fruition has been something of an epic journey.

Editing this book, and collecting together such a wealth of exceptional artwork, has given me the opportunity to embark on a truly global exploration of modern fantasy illustration. It has been a delightful, horizon-broadening expedition that, albeit for the most part undertaken in only electronic form via the Internet, has been nonetheless intrepid. It has enabled me to work with artists I've admired for many years, providing a great excuse to investigate the latest exciting projects of old friends and colleagues within the industry, and perhaps best of all, I discovered the work of a new wave of incredibly talented creators.

My search has brought me into contact with leading artists all over the world; across the U.S., Canada and South America, throughout Europe, Asia, and the Middle East. With such an international gathering, it's fascinating to observe the various differences, and perhaps more interestingly, the great many similarities of contemporary fantasy art that comes from different countries and cultures around the world.

The best fantasy art can provide a seductive escape route into a world of make believe; a way of blurring the borderline between the external reality we all share, and an artist's individual mental landscape. But a certain globalization of the high fantasy genre is apparent today; undoubtedly due to the widespread influence of fantasy films, computer games, and other popular media from Western Europe and the U.S. This often leads to artwork that conforms to accepted interpretations of over-familiar high fantasy themes.

Combined with this, painting styles also become extremely similar in the pursuit of fashionable effects, particularly in the field of concept design. Here, individualism can be obscured through the emulation of certain universally adopted fast-and-loose digital techniques, which can produce quick and effective, but sometimes anonymous, results. It's refreshing to encounter distinctive work that reflects an artist's unique cultural heritage and a wider frame of reference, and I hope I've presented some exciting examples of such work in *Pocket Fantasy Art*.

I've selected work from a broad spectrum of artists, some of whom are already extremely well-known and respected in fantasy art circles, some who are exciting rising stars well on their way to great success, and also from a range of brilliant new artists who, through this book, will see their art in print for the very first time. I'm delighted to have had the opportunity to bring together all these tremendously talented people and showcase their work, and working with each one has been an interesting experience. I think you'll agree that the book's combination of established fantasy artists and fresh new talent has resulted in an inspirational collection of fantastic imagery.

An interesting mixture of traditional and digital media is presented in the wide range of artwork on show in *Pocket Fantasy Art*. This reflects the degree to which the two disciplines currently coexist, but the widespread adoption of the digital approach will continue to increase as its advantages are obvious, particularly to busy illustrators with a need to speed up production time within tight deadlines, leveraging their natural talents and techniques. Many artists employ a workflow that utilizes elements of both, most commonly maintaining the spontaneity of sketching on paper, and then scanning to paint digitally. A software package like Corel Painter can emulate so many aspects of natural media successfully to be virtually indistinguishable from the real thing, and, with many paintings in this collection, you may find it is necessary to consult the caption to learn whether digital or traditional media has been used. As the digital medium matures, it's gaining something of its own aesthetic, as previous new media have done before it. The digital artwork in this collection heralds the new wave of contemporary creators and their endlessly adaptable new medium: the computer.

Many of the pieces presented here are brand new and exclusive to this volume. Other artwork comes from virtually every kind of fantasy-themed media, including book and graphic novel covers, role-playing games, and collectible card games. The material appears here uncropped and free from additional graphics, so in many cases it's the first time

the imagery can be seen the way the artist created it. Also showcased is concept and production art for computer games and film projects, which includes work not intended for print elsewhere; so many of these images are seen here for the very first time.

The role of an art book like this could conceivably be questioned in the modern digital age, given the prevalence of excellent online fantasy art galleries. From an artist's point of view, it's true that an effective personal website will ultimately provide them with more exposure, reaching a far larger potential audience than a book release is ever likely to achieve. Nevertheless, no matter how much wonderful artwork there is to view with ease online, it ultimately feels like a rather transitory interaction. No amount of Internet clicking quite equals the greater sense of permanence gained from the intimate, tactile experience of leafing through the glossy pages of a book which contains well-reproduced and carefully chosen examples of the best of a genre's art, and that has been our ambition with this volume.

Here, you will find some of the finest, freshest, and most exciting talents in the world of fantasy illustration, brought together in a dazzling array of artwork presented in one luxurious showcase volume. This is not a book of retrospectives, but examines what illustrators and painters are creating today in their approach to fantasy art, and represents them in a book that looks forward rather than back. The following pages are graced with some of the very best in contemporary fantasy art. This is fantasy art now!

◀ **Odin**
Glen Angus
Portfolio work
Adobe Photoshop

*This was created in the wake
of artwork Glen had done
for the new edition of the*
Dungeons & Dragons
Deities and Demigods
*book. "I was extremely lucky
to get to illustrate many of the
Norse Gods in the new book
but I wanted to do my own
interpretation of Odin as I
have always been fascinated
by all things Viking."*

◄ **"Thou Shall Not Pass!"**
Paul Bourne
Portfolio work
Daz Bryce and Corel Paint Shop Pro
www.contestedground.co.uk

*With this image, Paul wanted
to portray true bravery, as he
reveals: "The brave knight who
fights a dragon is not brave
if he is not afraid, but the
terrified knight who fights a
dragon shows genuine bravery
and strength of character. This
knight, who has clearly seen
some action already, confronts
the viewer, or an unseen
aggressor, outside the picture.
He is alone, and without the
protection of a helmet."*

▶ **Knights of Ansalon**
Jason Engle
Game book cover
Dragonlance:
Knightly Orders of Ansalon from
Margaret Weis Productions
www.jaestudio.com

Jason has worked in games
publishing for many years,
and has always been an avid
gamer. "Occasionally, I've
been lucky enough to get my
hands on a commission that
involves a game I played as
a child. This was one of those
occasions, and I can't stress
enough how refreshing it can
be to put your time and energy
into something that you already
have such a strong familiarity
with, and such a great sense of
inspirational nostalgia as well."

▶ **Solomon Kane**
Greg Staples
Movie poster illustration
Solomon Kane from Davis Films
Corel Painter
www.gregstaples.co.uk

This painting was created as a poster for a film festival, to promote the movie version of Robert E. Howard's Solomon Kane. *Greg was the concept artist on the project. While the film was in production, Greg said: "I've been working on the movie, doing concept art, production paintings, and this poster, which I produced for the Berlin film market. It's a great script, and I'm looking forward to seeing the finished film."*

◄ **The Golden Armor**
Felipe Machado Franco
Portfolio work
Adobe Photoshop
http://finalfrontier.thunderblast.net

*Felipe created this artwork as
a gift. "My girlfriend playfully
hinted that recently I hadn't
featured her in any artwork,
so I made something especially
that she would like. I started
with a photograph of her, taken
from a series of sword attack
poses. As the basis for the horse,
I used a photo of a sculpture,
and the armor was made from
simple shapes, carefully repeated
and shaded."*

◄ **Black Wolf Ronin**
Robert Chang
Portfolio work
Adobe Photoshop and Corel Painter
www.ethereality.info

*Robert describes this as a spur
of the moment idea, which he
then decided to render fully.
"I think part of the origin of
the idea was that I felt a little
guilty about mostly depicting
attractive females. But so far,
since this piece, I've not produced
any other paintings featuring
only male characters . . . I guess
I stopped feeling guilty! The
tattoo on his arm says, you
guessed it, 'Black Wolf.'"*

▶ **Fire and Water**
William O'Connor
Portfolio work
Oil on masonite
www.wocstudios.com

An illustration inspired by Tolkien's The Hobbit. *Bill sets the scene: "Bard, the captain of the guard, fires the last magic arrow at the rampaging Smaug. The lonely mountain looms in the background. The bird with the secret of Smaug's weakness watches as the arrow is about to be fired." The composition of this image is influenced by Japanese woodblock prints, and the limited palette infuses the painting with a sense of age and timelessness.*

◀ **Slaine**
Clint Langley
Book cover
Slaine: The Books of Invasions
Vol. 1 from Rebellion
Adobe Photoshop
www.clintlangley.com

Clint was commissioned by Rebellion to create this powerful cover. "I collaborated closely with the writer Pat Mills over four years, to create a cast of Celtic characters for Slaine, who fought it out over 300 pages of comic art. The three volumes chart my progression as an artist, representing some of my finest work."

◀ **Hard Day's Work**
Kory Heinzen
Portfolio work
Adobe Photoshop and LightWave 3D
http://korysdiner.homestead.com

*This painting illustrates a
short story that Kory has been
writing. "This image is the
first of these characters to be
been shown to the world. In
the aftermath of a battle, this
unlikely duo revel in victory.
As legendary mercenaries, they
wander the land; one fighting
for the money, one for the thrill.
Their reasons for fighting may
be different, but the results are
always the same; when their
swords are raised, armies will
fall. I painted this in Photoshop
over a rough 3D layout created
in Lightwave."*

▶ **Quag Keep**
J. P. Targete
Book cover
Quag Keep from BookSpan (SFBC)
www.targeteart.com

*J. P. explains that, as with
most artists, he normally
prefers to create an
underdrawing before starting
to paint, but, on this occasion,
he simply began by applying
color. "It was time consuming
because I was correcting all the
while as I painted, but it turned
out to be a lot of fun. Lately,
I've wanted to focus on facial
expressions, so I gave the main
warrior a really grim look, like
he's ready to jump right into
a fight."*

◄ **Silver**
Daryl Mandryk
Portfolio work
Adobe Photoshop
www.mandrykart.com

*Daryl has imagined a character,
conflicted somewhere between
good and evil; perhaps a good
character about to fall from
grace. "I invent a story about
a character as I work. What is
his function? How did he get
here? I try to work the answers
into the picture, in both subtle,
and not so subtle ways, giving
just enough so that the viewer's
imagination takes over and
crafts a story of their own."*

▶ **Riddler's Fayre 2**
Jeff Anderson
Book cover
Riddler's Fayre No.2
from Highland Books
Adobe Photoshop

Initially, Jeff was reluctant to adopt a digital way of working. "I had hoped digital art was a craze that wouldn't affect me, and that I could carry on painting traditionally. But eventually, I made the leap and loved it. It has been a slow process, but very rewarding. This is one of the first full pieces I've made, other than coloring some of my comic book line work."

▶ **Hunters**
Pascal Blanche
Portfolio work
Autodesk 3ds Max and
Adobe Photoshop
www.3dluvr.com/pascalb

*Pascal's very solid 3D figure
work is in direct homage to
the dynamic paintings of the
master of heroic fantasy, Frank
Frazetta, and is also inspired by
the powerful character designs
of Katsuya Terada. In turn,
Terada's distinctive rakugaki
style (the practice of drawing
constantly, everywhere and
anywhere) was influenced
by European artists such
as Moebius.*

◀ **White Tiger Clan**
Kerem Beyit
Game illustration
Hukumran Senfoni from
Sovereign Symphony
Adobe Photoshop
http://kerembeyit.gfxartist.com

A majestic white tiger makes
a truly powerful steed for this
fully armored samurai rider.
In Kerem's monochromatic
composition, the muted and
cool color palette conveys
the freezing surroundings
of a hostile mountain
environment, providing an
evocative backdrop for this
striking character concept.
The thick covering of snow in
the foreground is reflected in
the glinting, steely eyes of the
great beast, as it fixes them
hungrily upon the viewer.

► **Till Death Do Us Part**
Robert Chang
Magazine illustration for ImagineFX
Adobe Photoshop and Corel Painter
www.ethereality.info

*This piece was a work in
progress for years before Robert
completed it as a magazine
tutorial. However, this version
has been updated since being
published. "This painting
depicts a family of three being
hunted by demons; mother,
father, and baby. The parents
protect the baby with their
lives, while the demons conjure
dark magic, using the skull of
a fallen comrade as their source
of power. The father counters
the assault with his own magic,
channeled through his sword."*

◄ **Necro Warrior**
Rob Thomas
Portfolio work
Adobe Photoshop
www.mindsiphon.com

Rob describes how this piece was not created for any specific client, but painted entirely for fun. However, it was soon selected for an interesting commercial use: "I was contacted by the black metal band, Liche, who wanted to use it for the cover of their album **Within the Valley of Megiddo***. I was delighted to grant permission."*

▶ **Chi You and Taotie**
Xiao-chen Fu
Portfolio work
Adobe Photoshop
http://krishna-fu.cgsociety.org

*In this painting, Fu has portrayed Chi You,
a legendary leader and a powerful war deity
from ancient Chinese and Korean mythology.
Chi You is riding the fearsome Taotie; a creature
frequently depicted in bronze sculpture. Fu
explains more: "Chi You is a god of the Miao
people, and the Taotie is one of the biggest and
most evil of the ancient monsters. Taotie's body
is made of bronze, and he possesses a voracious
appetite. In a war with other gods, Chi You
summoned Taotie and rode him into battle."*

◄ **Bogatyr**
Michal Ivan
Book cover
Adobe Photoshop
http://perzo.cgsociety.org/about

*In his painting for a fantasy
novel book cover, Michal has
depicted a mighty Bogatyr, one
of the heroic warriors from epic
medieval Russian folk poems.
"This particular character is the
great hero Ilya Muromets, who
suffered serious illness in his
youth until he was miraculously
healed and given superhuman
strength, after which he became
the greatest of all the Bogatyrs."*

▶ **Magic Item**
Francis Tsai
Game book cover
Magic Item Compendium
from Wizards of the Coast
Adobe Photoshop
www.teamgt.com

*Wizards of the Coast wanted their cover to show
a character equipped with many different kinds
of magic items that are used in the* Magic Item
Compendium *role-playing game. Francis
explains, "The challenge I faced was to compose
all of the equipment in a way that didn't make
the character seem overly weighed down with
a lot of awkward gear."*

◀ **Ulk Rider**
Karl Richardson
Game illustration
Hordes: Evolution from
Privateer Press
Adobe Photoshop
www.epilogue.net/cgi/database/art/list.pl?gallery=14213

*The brief for this artwork was a fairly simple one
for Karl, in that he had to make sure both the rider
and his mount looked as sinister as possible. "This
wasn't difficult, as these particular characters have
deathly pale, angular features, and wear black
leather. I've done quite a number of the Legion of
Everblight to which this rider belongs, and must
admit they appeal to my darker side, which comes
to the fore, especially if I'm still working on them
at two in the morning!"*

◀ **Rostam**
Adel Adili
Portfolio work
Adobe Photoshop
www.adel3d.com

*In ancient Persian mythology,
Rostam is a legendary hero;
mightiest of Iranian paladins.
He became immortalized in the
10th century* Shahnameh *or*
Epic of Kings, *which contains
pre-Islamic folklore and
history. Similar to the legend of
Hercules, Rostam passes through
a hero's journey, called Rostam's
Seven Labors. Adel has chosen
to depict his Third Labor, which
involves the slaying of a dragon.*

▶ **Dark Knight**
Jason Engle
Book cover
Infernum: The Art of Jason Engle
from Paper Tiger
Adobe Photoshop
www.jaestudio.com

Jason painted this death-dealing, dark knight in homage to Frank Frazetta's work. "Frazetta has been an inspiration and catalyst throughout my career. As with most images, once you begin work it starts to shape itself. This figure was intended as that classic fantasy archetype, the villainous knight; so dark he becomes almost a silhouette against such a bright background. I worked with a limited palette, just like Frazetta would have often done."

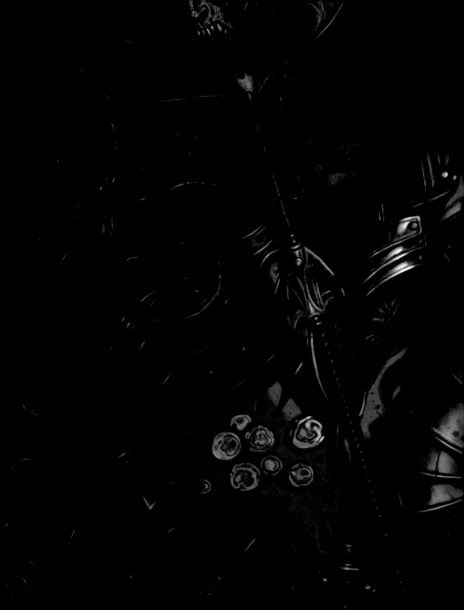

CHAPTER 2
WARRIOR WOMEN AND FEARLESS FEMALES

◄ **Eva in Repose**
R. K. Post
Promotional illustration
Dungeon Siege 2: Broken World
from Gas Powered Games
Adobe Photoshop
www.rkpost.net

*From a dramatic viewpoint
directly overhead, we see a
golden-armored warrior
maiden lying in a pool of
light. Surrounded by spilled
treasure and the slain bodies
of her many monstrous
foes, we assume she lies
injured or recovering,
after the prolonged and
bloody slaughter.*

► **Dragon Reflection**
Anne Stokes
Collectible card game illustration
Deck Armor from Max Protection
Adobe Photoshop
www.annestokes.com

The bold and attention-grabbing visual device that Anne set out to feature in her painting was this reflection of a dragon's glowing eye, shown in the mirror-like blade of a sword. The result is a simple, yet striking, image. Maybe the warrior has some affinity or symbiosis with this dragon, or maybe she's a dragon slayer. The artist wants to leave it to the viewer to decide.

◀ **Bone of the Ocean**
Jian Guo
Portfolio work
Corel Painter
http://breathing2004.gfxartist.com

*In this eerie, moonlit scene, Jian
has shown a seductive sea witch
standing within the huge rib
cage of a sea creature she's lured
to its death. Looming in the
background we see, silhouetted,
the rotting hulk of a wrecked
galleon, overpowered by her
dark magic. Signaling with
her flaming skull lantern, the
beguiling sea witch is intent
upon luring more seafarers to
their doom.*

▶ **End of Godliness**
Kuang Hong
Portfolio work
Adobe Photoshop
www.zemotion.net

*In Christianity, a fallen angel
is an angel that has been exiled
or banished from Heaven.
According to some traditions,
fallen angels will roam the
Earth until Judgment Day, when
they will be sent to Hell. This is
the state of exile in which Kuang
shows his angel character. "This
painting is about an angel that
is falling, and it is depicted
here on an earthly mountain
top. Carrying a bloodied cross,
the angel is hoping that a final
prayer can redeem its soul.
Alas, it has failed to escape the
eventual fate of the fallen."*

◄ **Dragon Skins**
Denise Garner
Portfolio work
Watercolor
www.towerwindow.com

*In this delicate watercolor, the viewer is presented
with the incongruous figure of a slight young
woman wearing the trophies of dragon slaying,
and brandishing a huge sword. Denise reveals more
about the painting: "The original piece was created
in transparent and opaque watercolor, on illustration
board. The purpose of the painting was to experiment
with various textures, and to juxtapose the feminine
with the somewhat violent. I created it specifically to
display at a world fantasy convention."*

Jaga
Michal Ivan
Book cover
Draci Carevna from
Wales Publishing
Adobe Photoshop
http://perzo.cgsociety.org/about

This painting by Michal was used for a novel based on Russian legends. "The picture depicts Baba Jaga in the shadowy world between life and death; a limbo full of gigantic saurians." In traditional Russian tales, Baba Jaga is a witch who flies through the air in a mortar, using the pestle as a rudder, and sweeping away her tracks with a broom of silver birch. In this portrayal, she looks a little different as she is depicted as young and athletic.

◄ **Dreamfall**
Jason Engle
Portfolio work
Adobe Photoshop
www.jaestudio.com

Every so often, inspiration can strike when it's least expected, and it sometimes comes from something as simple as composition, as Jason found. "Composition can be tricky, but it can also do amazing things. This image has a very pure composition: I kept detail and color to a minimum, and avoided most of the usual tricks used in fantasy art for adding high drama and action. But this still manages to create a scene that seems both dreamlike and enchanting in its own way."

▶ **Kill the Winter**
Xiao-chen Fu
Portfolio work
Adobe Photoshop
http://krishna-fu.cgsociety.org

Fu has created a heavily stylized portrayal of a goddess riding into battle. "She is Heyhu, the goddess who kills gods. Four gods once controlled the four seasons; the Winter God was the most powerful and capricious. For over 4,000 years he ruled, becoming mad with power until the seasons and weather were in disarray. Charging on her horse, Heyha cut off the head of the Winter God and the seasons returned to normal."

◀ **Shugenja**
Jon Hodgson
Collectible card game illustration
Legend of the Five Rings from
Alderac Entertainment Group
Adobe Photoshop and Corel Painter
www.jonhodgson.com

*Jon explains that he had a very
open brief for this image, and he
found it great fun to invent the
mountain setting. "It's a nice
change of pace to occasionally
paint something beautiful,
rather than a rotten zombie, or
a stinking goblin. I often work
in earth colors, so this one was
a nice change on that front as
well. Painter creates heavy paint
marks well, and as the digital
medium matures, it's gaining
something of its own aesthetic,
as previous new mediums have
also done."*

▶ **Scarlet Mage**
Anne Stokes
Private commission
Adobe Photoshop
www.annestokes.com

*This image was commissioned
privately from Anne to
immortalize a gamer's cherished
player character. "It was fun
to design the costume, and
I'm especially pleased with her
dragon boots. The subtle blues
in the background are designed
to contrast with the bright
red of the mage's clothing,
and the brewing storm adds
to the drama of her imminent
spell-casting."*

◄ **Scythe Wolf**
Robert Chang
Portfolio work
Adobe Photoshop and
Corel Painter
www.ethereality.info

*This painting took Robert a long time to complete
due to its high level of detail: "I really should switch
to a more relaxed style that isn't so highly rendered.
The dress was especially hard to paint, and I had
to study a lot of satin and silk references to get it
right. The wolves took a long time too, but were
much easier in comparison, after studying a lot
of reference material."*

▶ **Spellsword**
Sacha "Angel" Diener
Portfolio work
Adobe Photoshop
www.angel3d.ch

Angel has depicted a fearless
elfin warrior maiden, striding
through a lost kingdom. He
describes the background
story he invented: "A curse has
plunged this emerald valley
into darkness, with its long-
dead inhabitants resurrected
as rotting creatures that are
neither alive nor dead. For years
no-one has dared enter this evil
place, until a lone elf, ready
to face all danger, enters the
haunted mists, her Spellsword
slicing through the fog."

CHAPTER 3
MYTHS AND MONSTERS

◀ **Dragon Rider**
Matthew Bradbury
Portfolio work
Adobe Photoshop
*www.epilogue.net/cgi/data-
base/art/list.pl?gallery=11601*

"*In the flying beast there is
some influence from* The
Lord of the Rings *films,
particularly the aerial
sequences in* The Return
of the King, *but I took the
most pleasure in painting
the background. I've always
admired the work of matte
painters, with Dylan Cole's
film work proving especially
inspiring, and so I chose a
very cinematic aspect ratio.*"

► **Minotaur**
Carlos Cabrera
Portfolio work
Corel Painter
www.carloscabrera.com.ar

*Having always loved the story
of Theseus, Carlos was inspired
to paint a Minotaur. In Greek
mythology, the Minotaur
was a creature that was part
man and part bull, to whom
young Athenians were sent to
be devoured. It dwelled at the
center of a gigantic labyrinth
built for King Minos of Crete,
near his palace in Knossos.
Specially built to hold the
Minotaur, the huge maze
was designed by the architect
Daedalus, and the ferocious but
rather unfortunate creature was
eventually slain by Theseus with
the help of Ariadne. "Minotaur"
is Greek for "Bull of Minos."*

◄ **Yobanjin Wyrm**
Jon Hodgson
Collectible card game illustration
Legend of the Five Rings from
Alderac Entertainment Group
Adobe Photoshop and
Corel Painter
www.jonhodgson.com

*This game world is a deep and
inspiring one, as well as being
extremely popular. It demands
some thought when adding to it,
as Jon describes: "I had a great
time designing this creature. I
took inspiration from Chinese
dragon dancers, and tried to
work backward from their
stylized look, to something 'real.'
I like to bring as much real
world texture to my work as
I can, and have a huge stock
of handmade textures on file."*

◀ **Zombie Psycho**
Greg Staples
Collectible card game illustration
Magic: The Gathering from Wizards
of the Coast
Corel Painter
www.gregstaples.co.uk

*Greg is perhaps best known
for his paintings for* Magic:
The Gathering, *and for his
dynamic work in comic books.
His art for* Judge Dredd
*marked the beginning of his
career as an illustrator, and
since then he has painted some
of the most popular comic book
characters, including Spider-
Man and Batman. He has also
worked on many other projects,
including* War of the Worlds
with Jeff Wayne.

▶ **Mountain Dragons**
Leo Hartas
Book illustration
Dragonquest from Fernleigh Books
Adobe Photoshop and Corel Painter
www.hartas.eclipse.co.uk

*Leo describes how his brief for
this piece was very open. "The
idea was a puzzle picture, with
a lot of dragons to count; some
hidden and difficult to find.
The challenge of composing
so many dragons was to
avoid the image turning into
a messy 'dragon soup,' so I
broke it up into the classic
foreground, middle ground,
and distance composition, to
create an illusion of depth. My
inspiration for the vertical rock
forms came from photos I've
seen of incredible limestone
spires; aspects of nature that
seem more fantastical than
any fantasy."*

▶ **The Last Guardian**
Jian Guo
Portfolio work
Corel Painter
http://breathing2004.gfxartist.com

*An arcane library is the setting
for this clash between might
and magic. Jian has depicted a
colossal, demonic figure, molten
drool dripping from its fiery
maw, its hunched form taut with
sinewy power. One enormous
apelike arm has crashed to the
floor, dwarfing the magician in
the foreground, and highlighting
the difference in scale. This is
further intensified by the low
point of view behind and
below the human figure.*

◄ **Byakhee**
Tony Hough
Portfolio work
Gouache on board
www.tonyhough.co.uk

Tony has long been inspired by
the Cthulhu Mythos *tales of*
H. P. Lovecraft, and the Byakhee
are a race of interstellar beings
that feature in Lovecraft's story,
The Festival. *"There flapped*
rhythmically a horde of tame,
trained, hybrid winged things . . .
not altogether crows, nor moles,
nor buzzards, nor ants, nor
decomposed human beings, but
something I cannot, and must
not, recall."

▶ **The Watchmaker**
Matthew Bradbury
Portfolio work
Adobe Photoshop
www.epilogue.net/cgi/database/art/
list.pl?gallery=11601

*A masked fiend offers us this
watch, about which Matthew
tells all: "I imagined this
guy as a guardian of time
and causality. If you possess
knowledge of certain dark
arts, you might have the skill
to summon him, and he would
present you with a watch. This
watch would allow you free
movement through time. The
catch is, if you upset the course
of history, he will return to
reclaim his property and deliver
a terrible punishment."*

◄ **Realms of Sorcery**
Ralph Horsley
Game book cover
Realms of Sorcery from
Games Workshop
Acrylic
www.ralphhorsley.co.uk

This image provided a challenge for Ralph because it was going to be used as a wraparound cover, as he describes: "This meant that the right half needed to work as a front cover, as well as part of the whole. Likewise, the left half was going to have text placed over it, and so required less detail. To make the red demon pop out, I chose a green shade for the background. These contrasting colors hopefully work to really make the cover appear prominent and attention-grabbing on the shelf."

► **Temple of Terror**
Martin McKenna
Book cover
Temple of Terror from Wizard Books
Adobe Photoshop
www.martinmckenna.net

The idea for this piece was simply to show an extreme closeup of a goblin in pore-probing detail. To achieve the photorealistic feel of the face, painting was combined with areas of texture taken from macro photos of a model's skin. In a digital skin graft, the patches of flesh texture were placed on the face, incorporated and blended in, merging with painted areas. Adding to the photographic feel is the soft blurring around the edges of the portrait, to suggest a little depth of field.

◀ **Blood of the Dragon**
Clint Langley
Book cover
Blood of the Dragon courtesy of
The Black Library/Games Workshop
Limited (www.black-library.com).
Copyright Games Workshop Ltd
2006. Used with permission.
Adobe Photoshop
www.clintlangley.com

*Clint built this monster using
textures that were created in
Photoshop and then formed
into the dragon. "Once the
composition and mood looked
right, I started to sculpt the
details using a Wacom Stilos,
much the same as completing
an oil painting. The texture
on the dragon's fire gives the
whole image a more painted
look, which I try to capture
throughout my art."*

▶ **Guenhwyvar**
Julia Alekseeva
Portfolio work
Adobe Photoshop
http://julax.ru

This image was inspired by the Forgotten Realms *books by R. A. Salvatore. As Julia explains, "The books' visuals really grabbed me, with their weird underground realm and its fabulous denizens. I painted scenes directly from the books, visualizing all the descriptive details as I imagined them. I've now produced a series of eleven paintings inspired by the stories."*

◀ **Ice Dragon**
Yvonne Gilbert
Book cover
Colored pencil
www.yvonnegilbert.com

*A little girl clings with delight
to the crisp, frozen mane
of this ice dragon as it flies
through the glittering, moonlit
night. Yvonne has shown the
creature's cold breath turning
immediately to solid ice as it
streams behind its head, upon
which are horns shaped from
the upstanding spikes of icicles.
The outline of the dragon's form
is defined against the night sky
by a shimmering halo of frost.*

▶ **Cupid and Psyche**
Rebecca Guay
Portfolio work
Oil over gouache on paper
www.rebeccaguay.com

Rebecca reveals this to be a personal favorite, from a series of mythologically themed works. "Since childhood, I've been obsessed with this story. The journey and trials for love and trust, and the deeply passionate subtext of sensuality, have been at the root of my inspirations as an artist. I've always wanted to illustrate this story, to show the moment just before the first kiss, and to capture the mystery and energy of that elusive, precious moment."

◀ **Temptation**
Denise Garner
Portfolio work
Watercolor and gouache
www.towerwindow.com

This painting was a challenging
work for Denise to complete to
her satisfaction, as she recalls.
"The subject evolved over a
number of weeks, and part of
the process included a strong
desire to throw the thing in the
trash! I originally concentrated
on the figure, filling in the
rest of the scenery as I went.
Ultimately, what I enjoy most
about the picture is its softness
and color harmony."

▶ **Daphne & Apollo**
Adel Adili
Portfolio work
Autodesk 3ds Max and
Adobe Photoshop
www.adel3d.com

Adel rendered this amorous
vignette, based on a story from
Greek mythology. Daphne was
Apollo's first love, brought
about by the malice of Cupid
who fired two arrows, a sharp
one of gold to excite love, the
other of blunt lead to repel love.
With the leaden shaft, he struck
the nymph Daphne, and with
the golden one, Apollo, through
his heart. Apollo was seized with
love for the maiden, but she
abhorred him, and to escape
his advances, she changed into
a laurel tree.

◄ **The Last Tarot**
Cyril Van Der Haegen
Portfolio work
Adobe Photoshop and
Corel Painter
www.tegehel.org

*This painting was originally
intended as a black and white
interior illustration for a role-
playing game release, but Cyril
took the design further, as he
describes: "I fell in love with the
concept, so for my own pleasure,
I decided to work it up as a full
color painting. I worked on it
primarily using Painter, but
with finishing touches and final
adjustments in Photoshop."*

◀ **Spawning Ground**
John Garner
Portfolio work
Acrylic
www.shadowsofthunder.com

*This painting, like much
of John's work, combines
astronomical themes with
classic fantasy elements.
"This piece was done by hand,
entirely in acrylics, with no
digital enhancement. I used
an airbrush to paint much
of the background, create the
atmospheric effects, and finally
add the highlights. Many thin
layers of paint were used to
create the shadows and slowly
work up to the highlights."*

▶ **Eye of the Dragon**
Martin McKenna
Book cover
Eye of the Dragon from Wizard Books
Adobe Photoshop
www.martinmckenna.net

*Not straying very far for
inspiration from the title of the
book, in this picture we stare
straight into a dragon's eyeball.
With only a small area of the
head around the eye to play
with, the challenge here was to
indicate reasonably clearly that
this was actually a dragon we
are close to, and not some other
scaly monster. Helping to convey
this is the suggestion of a great
spiny mass disappearing into
the shadows, and the inclusion
of the smoking nostrils.*

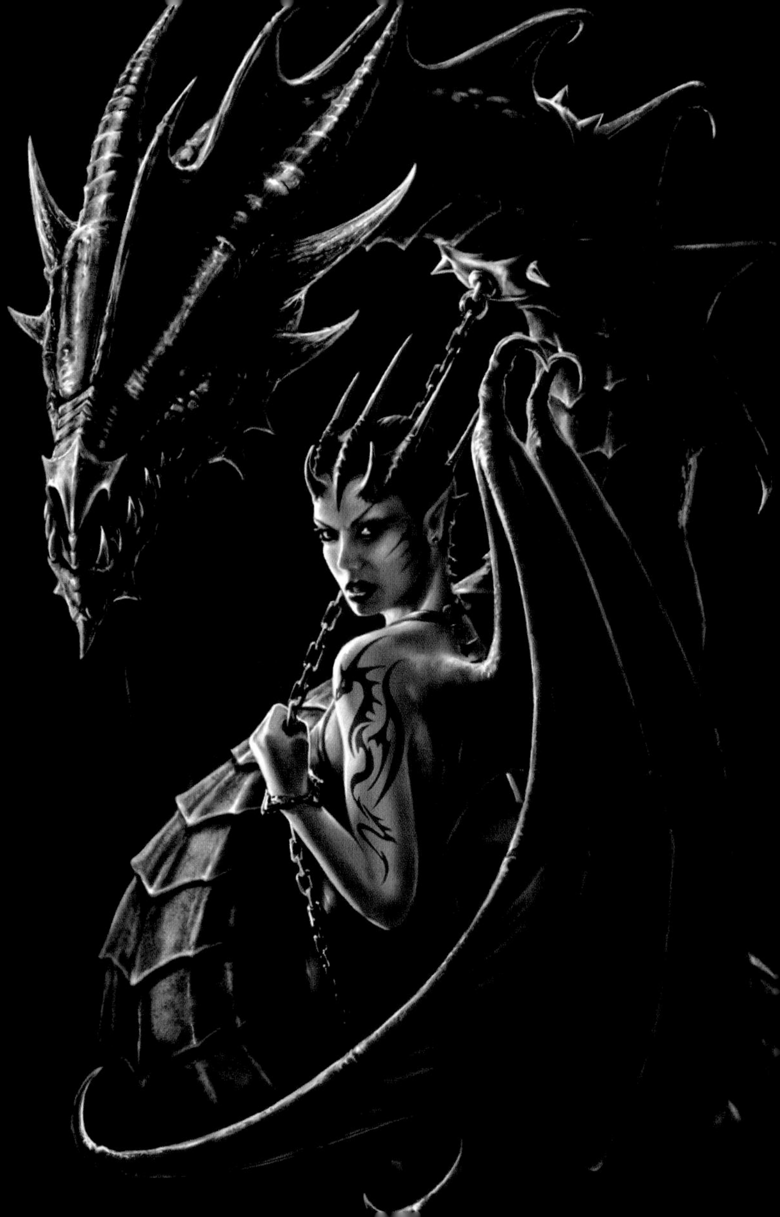

◄ **Controller**
Anne Stokes
T-shirt design for Spiral Direct Ltd
Adobe Photoshop
www.annestokes.com

*Anne painted this exotic female
with her dragon pet for the*
Dark Wear *range of T-shirts;
hence the strong design element
of the image, intended to work
when printed on black fabric.*
"*The curl of the dragon's body
is mirrored by the curve on
the female's wings. A dragon
can make for a useful pet, but
you had better make sure you're
in control.*"

▶ **Krike Dragon**
Kevin Crossley
Portfolio work
Adobe Photoshop
www.kevcrossley.com

*Kevin's spindly dragon recalls
aspects of John Tenniel's
Jabberwock illustration for*
Through the Looking Glass.
*"The underdrawing was a very
detailed pencil study, produced
in my usual haphazard
way. I then scanned this and
used Photoshop exclusively
during the painting process.
I incorporated photographs
of rust, lichen, scuffed metal,
and other textures into the
composition, using a variety
of blending modes and levels
of transparency, as well as
selective erasing."*

◀ **Ulysse**
Benjamin Carre
Book cover
Odyssée, les Naufragés
de Poséidon from
Père Castor-Flammarion
Adobe Photoshop
www.blancfonce.com

For this cover illustration,
Benjamin has imagined a truly
impressive reinvention of a
Cyclops. In Greek mythology,
the Cyclops is a member of a
primordial race of giants, each
with a single eye in the middle of
its forehead; seen here emitting
a powerful light beam. The
massive scale of this colossus is
cleverly conveyed through the
detail of the flock of birds, tiny at
this distance, that have perched
on the giant's shoulders.

▶ **Beauty and the Unicorn**
Rebecca Guay
Magazine cover
Cricket Magazine from
Carus Publishing
Gouache on paper
www.rebeccaguay.com

*In traditional folklore,
the unicorn is said to be
tameable only by a virgin
woman. A gentle and pensive
virgin has the power to attract
the unicorn, and one method
of hunting it involved
entrapment by a maiden.
Rebecca's painting suggests
a more innocent encounter.
"For me, this is my perfectly
pastoral piece. I wanted to
give a sense of light and the
ocean. I love the affection
between these totally mythical
archetypes; a unicorn and a girl
who is a sea maiden; a nymph
representing innocence."*

◀ **Elemental Moon**
Rick Sardinha
Game book cover
Elemental Moon from
Necromancer Games
Oil on masonite
www.battleduck.com

*Rick produced this painting
for the gaming supplement
of the same name. "For this
assignment, I chose to illustrate
a water elemental. I planned
this work around the close
association of the female
with life. The fluid nature
of the quasi-human female
anatomy emphasizes this, as
does the object floating above
one of her hands. It is a loose
representation of the Venus
of Willendorf, a prehistoric
fertility symbol."*

▶ **City of Peril**
Ralph Horsley
Game book cover
Fantastic Locations from
Wizards of the Coast
Acrylic
www.ralphhorsley.co.uk

*A swarming rat horde in a
moonlit urban setting was
the brief for Ralph's painting.
"I decided to go for a low point
of view so that the wererat
antagonists would loom over the
viewer. Along with the off-kilter
horizon line, this helps to create a
sense of menace, and reinforces
the feeling of being inside an
open sewer in the shadowy
depths of the city. The moon acts
as a focal point to draw in the
eye, and it also enabled me to
use back lighting to define the
figures and all those rats."*

◄ **Spell Breaker**
Martin McKenna
Book cover
Spellbreaker from Wizard Books
Adobe Photoshop
www.martinmckenna.net

*The brief for this cover was to
show a demonic figure stepping
out of a fiery pit. The suggestion
is that this is perhaps a gateway
leading from some infernal
dimension, or maybe an opened
casket that had magically
trapped the creature, from
which it's now breaking free.
I wanted the figure to be dark,
almost a silhouette in places,
particularly the head, to allow
the glowing eyes to stand out.*

◀ **Thor, Ultimate**
Glen Angus
Game illustration
Marvel Ultimate Alliance from
Marvel, Activision, and Ravensoft
Adobe Photoshop

*This image was created by
Glen as a character concept and
loading screen for a computer
game. "I wanted to paint Thor
as a weathered and hardened,
larger-than-life figure. I focused
on the hard planes of his face,
and the confident glare in his
eyes. Ironically, in the end, the
client wanted a gentler-looking
Thunder God, one closer to the
current Ultimates comic book
character. I kept this version for
my portfolio because it captures
my first instinct."*

▶ **Dunhuang**
Camille Kuo
Portfolio work
Oils and Adobe Photoshop
http://camilkuo.com/main.htm

*Inspired by a trip to Dunhuang
in China, Camille explains that
she painted this figure without
using the model reference she
normally employs. Painting
freely from her imagination
enabled her to keep the work
spontaneous and unconstrained
by any reference material that,
in pursuit of tightly detailed
realism, she feels can sometimes
impose limitations upon her
work. The background was
painted traditionally in oils
and scanned.*

◀ **The Disciplinant**
Kuang Hong
Portfolio work
Corel Painter
www.zemotion.net

*Using very traditional painting
techniques with Painter, and
applying individual brushstrokes
to no more than a single layer
was a time-consuming process
for Kuang. "This is a concept
piece based on a story of a
famous Chinese opera actor
who was murdered, and this is
a manifestation of his soul. The
control of the whole entity comes
from the white light at its center;
the body below and the huge
prop on top are merely tools
controlled by it."*

▶ **Minotaur**
Simon Dominic Brewer
Portfolio work
Corel Painter
www.painterly.co.uk

*Simon explains that he has
always been fascinated by
Greek mythology, and this is
his first attempt to depict the
battle between Theseus and the
Minotaur. "I wanted to portray
the Minotaur as being more
primal and fearsome than
simply a guy with a bull's head,
hence the more fundamental
combination of human and
animal. In Painter, I used
custom oils, acrylics, and chalk,
leaving some areas rough to
add dynamism. I also used
the slanted viewpoint for a
similar effect."*

▶▶ **Tales from the High Seas**
Patrick Reilly
Portfolio work
Adobe Photoshop
http://preilly.deviantart.com/gallery

*An atmospheric local pub
frequented by Patrick inspired
this piece. "The place had a very
old and creepy nautical feel,
with lime green lighting that
really caught my attention. It
was tiny and felt a lot like being
in the belly of an old pirate ship,
and as I was sipping my beer,
I expected a giant tentacle to
come crashing in."*

◀ **The Last Days**
Matthew Bradbury
Portfolio work
Adobe Photoshop
www.epilogue.net/cgi/database/art/
list.pl?gallery=11601

Matthew's vision offers a glimpse of a hell on earth in which a doomed Tyrannosaurus struggles to survive. "Dinosaurs might not be considered 'fantasy' creatures, but for me they hold as much fascination as any dragon of legend, perhaps even more so, as these giants really did live and breathe. This image is set at a time after the meteor impact, which almost certainly brought about their eventual extinction. I tried to imagine the harshest of environments, featuring poisoned skies above volcanic and geological mayhem."

▶ **Prophecy**
Benjamin Carre
Book cover
La Symphonie Des Siecles II: Prophecy from Pygmalion
Adobe Photoshop
www.blancfonce.com

In a subterranean lair, this golden dragon protectively encircles a young woman, who leans nonchalantly against its wing. Benjamin has made very effective use of the warm lighting from behind, to render the semiopaque quality of the dragon's membranous wings. The air sparkles with golden embers, and the ribbed nature of the cavern walls suggests this might even be the insides of a far more enormous creature.

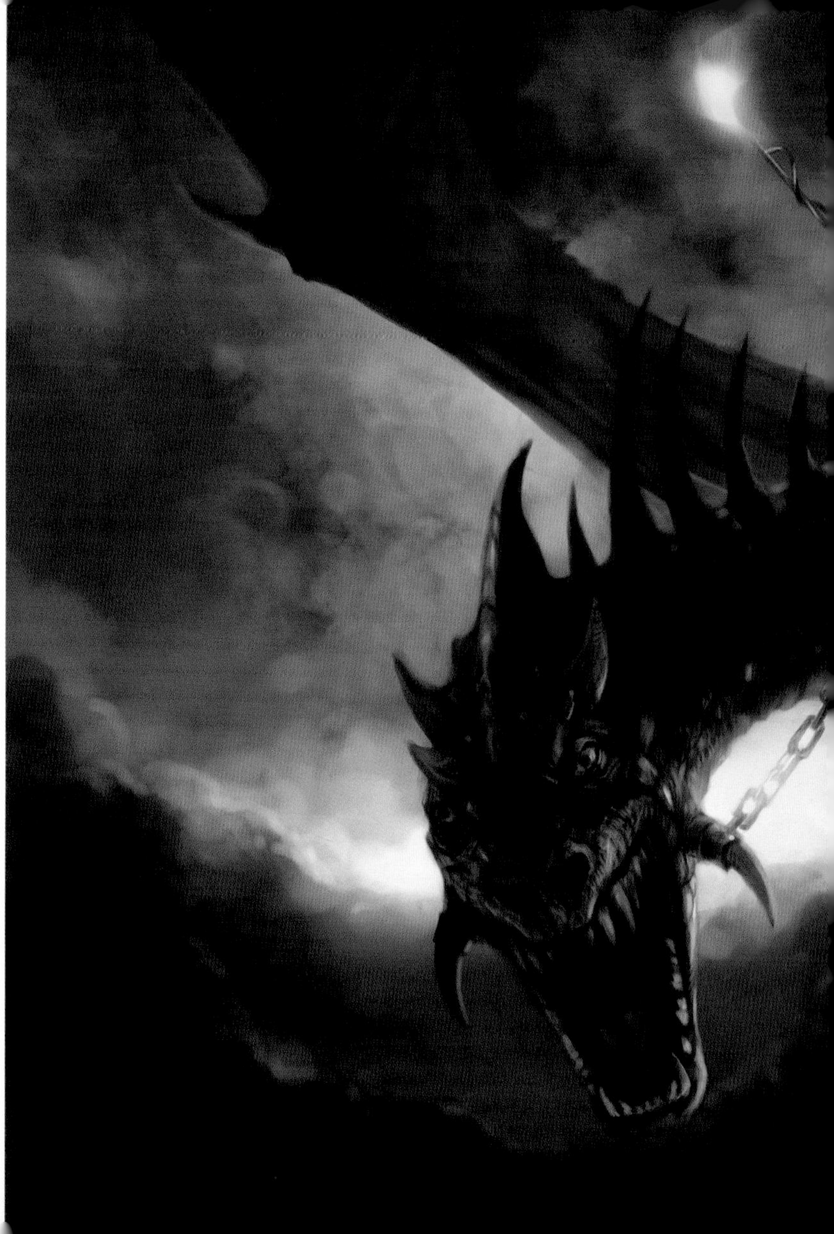

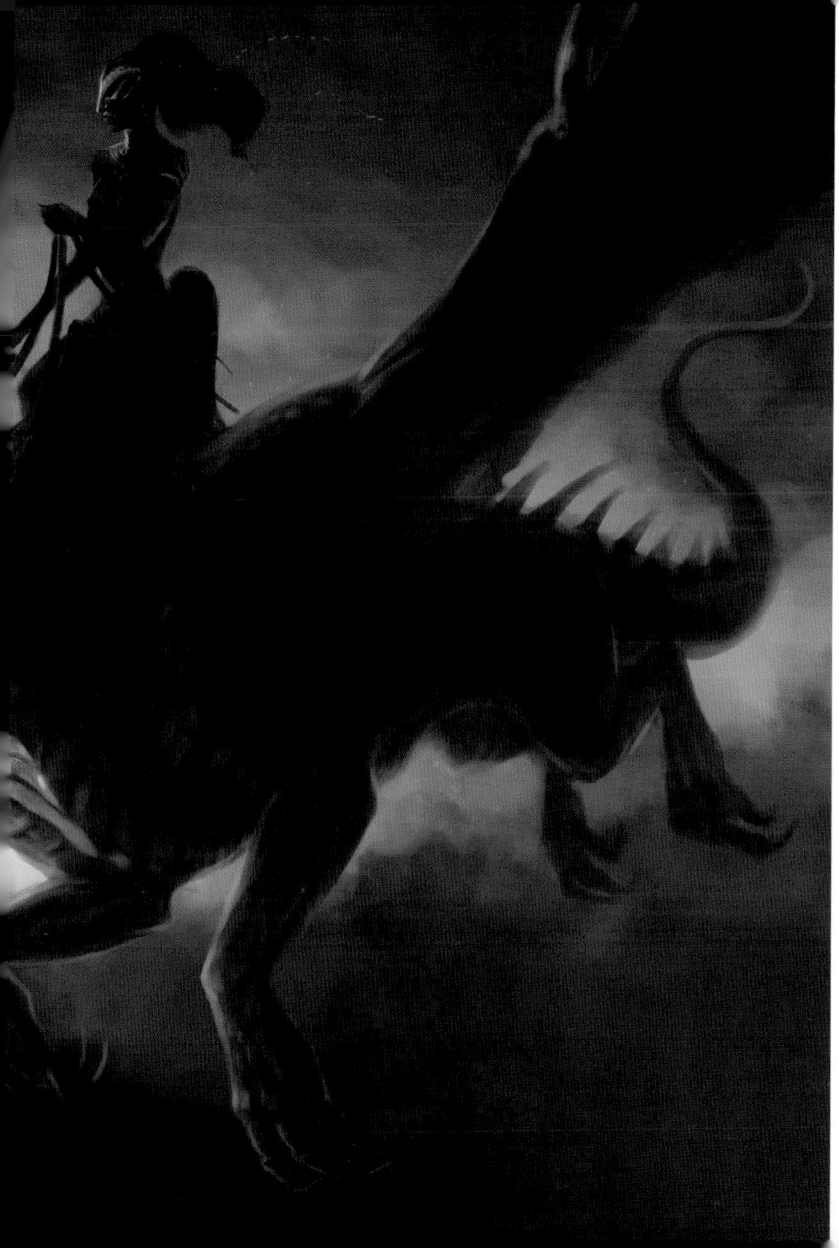

◀ **Dragon's World**
Julia Alekseeva
Collectible card game illustration
Berserk from Fantasy World
Publishing, Inc
Adobe Photoshop
http://julax.ru

*Julia has depicted a masked
female rider, holding her flaming
crop aloft as she steers her dragon
mount through storm clouds.
"In this work, I wanted to convey
the power of a mighty dragon,
deftly controlled and managed
by the spiritual forces of a fragile
enchantress. The dark world
inhabited by this dragon and
its rider is murky, but the skies
crackle with magic."*

▶ **Mighty Dragon**
Uwe Jarling
Portfolio work
Corel Painter
www.jarling-arts.com

*Uwe created this piece for his
ongoing* Mystical Creatures
*series of paintings. "I chose
to portray the centralized
beast from a low point of view
to increase its impact and
power, and for focus, I kept
the background simple and
uncluttered. I love to depict
legendary creatures of traditional
European folklore and myth.
Almost all of my work is created
digitally now, but I'm keen to
preserve the look of traditional
oil paintings."*

◄ **Tiltadron**
Mike Corriero
Portfolio work
Adobe Photoshop
www.mikecorriero.com

*The main focus of this
creature concept was to design
an asymmetrical giant. To
accentuate the asymmetry, Mike
decided to substitute one of its
legs with an arm, shrinking its
other limbs to vestigial forms.
The resulting figure appears
blasphemously twisted and
mutated, but incongruous
landscape features suggest the
creature has its origins firmly
rooted in nature. The warrior
figure provides scale, and wears
asymmetrical armor that echoes
the form of his titanic beast.*

▶ **Cerebrus**
Camille Kuo
Portfolio work
Adobe Photoshop
http://camilkuo.com/main.htm

*In Greek mythology, Cerberus
was the demon of the pit that
guarded the gates of Hades,
ensuring that all spirits could
enter, but none could return.
Traditionally depicted as a
monstrous three-headed hound,
here we see Cerberus in a much
more alluring human form.
Camille reveals that she posed
for the figure herself, and is
shown standing before the
hellgate, the key to which hangs
on a chain around her neck.*

◀ **Honey Queen**
Bryan Beaux Beus
Portfolio work
Corel Painter
www.beauxpaint.com

Bryan found inspiration for this painting in Grimm's Fairy Tales. "To lift a curse, our hero must guess which of three sleeping beauties is a princess. The only clue is that the young princess loved honey. Unable to solve the puzzle, he summons the Honey Queen who turns into a bumblebee, and tastes the sleepers' lips to see which has eaten honey. I've shown the Honey Queen hurrying to the castle upon her flying bear."

▶ **Claw Clan**
Kerem Beyit
Portfolio work
Adobe Photoshop
http://kerembeyit.gfxartist.com

Proud members of this leonine warrior clan pose beneath their tribal banner. Kerem has provided the figures with subtle but distinctive indications of individual character. Each warrior wears his mane slightly differently, with personal touches including plaits. A neat visual connection has been made between the creatures and the medieval lion, rampant heraldic devices just visible on their armor.

◄ **Keeper of the Fields**
Mike Corriero
Portfolio work
Adobe Photoshop and
Corel Painter
www.mikecorriero.com

The collapse of an industrialized society is glimpsed in this fall scene. Mike gives us more of his story: "The Keeper was once a hard-working machine that watched over the fields and crops, but it has now been abandoned. Low on energy and slowly rusting away, it sits watching the crows that mock it. This melancholy robot figure is also a small nod to the Tin Man in The Wizard of Oz.*"*

▶ **Wererats**
Jim Pavelec
Game book cover
Complete Guide to Wererats
from Goodman Games
Oil on paper on masonite
www.jimpavelec.com

The U.S. gaming company Goodman Games commissioned Jim to produce this book cover, and he chose to depict nocturnal were-creatures prowling on city rooftops by the light of a full moon. "The art director is really generous about giving artists creative freedom, so I was able to do pretty much whatever I wanted with this piece."

◄ **Wrecking Crew**
Patrick Reilly
Portfolio work
Adobe Photoshop
http://preilly.deviantart.com/gallery

Wanting to create something in the style of the old masters of high fantasy painting, such as Frank Frazetta, and inspired by sequences in The Lord of the Rings, *Patrick painted this scene populated with traditional, dark, fairy tale characters. To reproduce the look of an oil composition, Patrick decided to use mainly traditional painting techniques, and chose to paint everything on a single Photoshop layer.*

► **Majestic Dignity**
Uwe Jarling
Portfolio work
Corel Painter
www.jarling-arts.com

One of an ongoing series of paintings showcasing mythical creatures, Uwe has captured the free spirit of a unicorn in this picture. "I wanted to show the unicorn as prominently as possible, so I chose to have it rearing up on a hilltop. The low viewpoint helps to make the animal more impressive."

◀ **Night**
Richard Hescox
Portfolio work
Oil on canvas
www.richardhescox.com

This painting incorporates strong use of allegory, as Richard divulges: "I make use of the human form to symbolize and personify some aspect of nature, and this is one of a series of paintings I am working on in which I am exploring the grandeur and mystery of the landscape, and the natural forces that perform upon that stage."

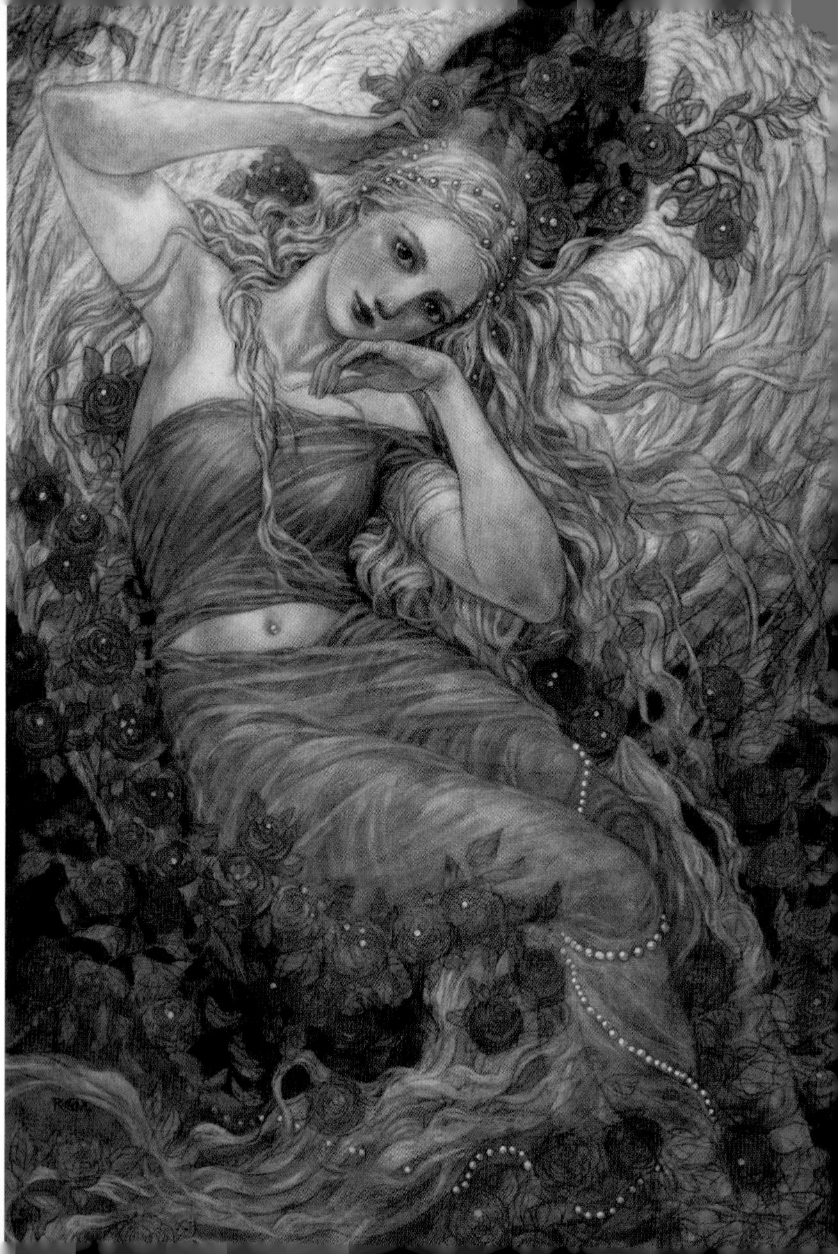

◀ **Angel of First Love**
Rebecca Guay
Game illustration
Angel Quest from
Angel Quest, Inc
Oil over gouache on panel
www.rebeccaguay.com

Rebecca describes how this painting contains the themes of love and passion that she finds forever appealing. "I wanted to paint a portrait that would feel like the face of love, and the embodiment of falling in love. I wanted her to be sensual, yet innocent, wide-eyed and absorbing, while maintaining a distant air. She is complete in her confidence and strength, and, although an angel, entirely earthly."

◀ **Siren Song**
Nick Harris
Portfolio work
Corel Painter

Dividing this scene into fore, mid, and background, to keep control over the tonal values, Nick then blocked everything in using the oil pastel variant in Painter, and applied shadows with digital tinting brushes. "I added detail, such as pattern interest, to the siren's tail using the Large Chalk variant with swirling paper textures. It all looked too bright and cheery, so I applied a blue Multiply layer and painted glows and glints into it with a light orange hue."

▶ **Day Dreamer**
Tony Hayes
Portfolio work
Autodesk 3ds Max, Adobe Photoshop, and e frontier Poser
www.my-art-gallery.co.uk

Tony's intention for this piece was to create a restful, placid image. "I enjoy creating pictures that get the viewer thinking, and I offer no clues as to how or why she is there. The basic 3D scene is little more than a rectangular wall with a tube set into it, built and textured in 3ds Max. The cloth was created by photographing a bed sheet, and using pillows under it to simulate the shape of the sleeping character's body."

◄ **Black Dandy**
Linda Tso
Book cover
Hotu Publishing
Adobe Photoshop
www.epilogue.net/cgi/database/art/
list.pl?gallery=8270

To paint this book cover, Linda needed to depict a necromancer who could raise the dead to join the legions of her zombie army. As Linda describes, "I thought it would be interesting to contrast a cheerful-looking and attractive girl with dark horror elements. For this painting, I finished a detailed grayscale tonal image first, then tinted it with color on separate layers."

▶ **Backdoor to Luxuriance**
Michael Zancan
Portfolio work
Oil on canvas
http://zancan.fr

Michael reveals that the word "luxuriance" had been repeating in his head for days like a leitmotif, and that the most natural response for him was to externalize it in paint. "To enable a brighter light to fall upon the hand, the whole painting had to be plunged in a subtle penumbra. After working out the body language with a live model, I tried to describe in the girl's face an expression of joyful surprise, mixed with a hint of worry."

◄ **As Holy as They Come**
Felipe Machado Franco
Portfolio work
Adobe Photoshop
http://finalfrontier.thunderblast.net

*Felipe feels it's important
to maintain his output of
personal work, in addition to
commissions from clients. "My
usual process is to start with a
photo shoot; in this particular
case, a nude model because I
intended to dress her digitally.
This is the best way to create
clothing that really fits the form.
I created each piece of armor
separately and assembled them
along her limbs. Working on a
grayscale version of the image,
I finally added lighting, color,
and texture."*

▶ **Flames of Magic**
Sacha "Angel" Diener
Portfolio work
Adobe Photoshop
www.angel3d.ch

*In this painting, Angel
has portrayed his sorceress
character, Elfborn, a dragon
woman and mistress of
elemental magic. "I've imagined
that in ages past there were
people able to manipulate the
very essence of what surrounds
us. Controlled by mind and soul,
the spiritual energy of nature
manifested and became what
was known as the 'flames of
magic.' This is a sketch I colored
fast and loose, trying to retain
the dynamic movement and raw
power of the initial sketch."*

◀ **Mev**
Rebecca Guay
Private commission
Pencil and gouache on paper
www.rebeccaguay.com

*This was a rare private
commission accepted by
Rebecca. "I agreed to paint this
because I felt very connected to
the strength of the character;
I've always loved warrior
women. She is beautiful and
strong, and went through
fundamental, life-altering
transformations, that appealed
to me on many levels. To pursue
art is an all-encompassing
daily endeavor of passion.
It's a glorious journey, full of
narcotic-like highs and lows,
and I'm most successful when
I feel that I've given some
important part of myself
to the image."*

▶ **What I See**
Melanie Delon
Portfolio work
Adobe Photoshop and Corel Painter
www.melaniedelon.com

*This romantic, yet mournful
scene illustrates a sad tale
described by Melanie: "Naery
was just a child when her
parents were killed during an
attack on their city. The king of
this land saved her and raised
her as his own daughter. Years
have passed, and despite all of
the king's love, she always feels
alone. Sometimes she lingers in
the ruin of her parents' home,
remembering her childhood."*

◀ **Benrig Medb**
R. K. Post
Collectible card game illustration
Anachronism for the History Channel
Adobe Photoshop
www.rkpost.net

*Medb is queen of Connacht
in the Ulster Cycle of Irish
mythology. Her father was
Eochaid Feidlech, the High King
of Ireland. The cycle consists
of about eighty stories, the
centerpiece of which is a battle
in which Medb invades Ulster at
the head of a huge army. R. K.'s
portrait of Medb features closely
observed Iron Age jewellery and
weapon designs, and he adds,
"This is one of a few pieces that
I have done based on historical
figures, although Medb is a bit
more on the mythical, folklore
side of things."*

▶ **Lady of Shalott**
Yvonne Gilbert
Portfolio work
Colored pencil
www.yvonnegilbert.com

Yvonne was inspired by a romantic poem by Alfred, Lord Tennyson. The poem, with its Arthurian subject matter, is loosely based on a story from Thomas Malory's Le Morte d'Arthur, *concerning Elaine of Astolat, a maiden who falls in love with Lancelot but dies of grief when he cannot return her love. The poem was particularly popular among artists of the Pre-Raphaelite movement, who shared Tennyson's interest in Arthurian legend, and their style is echoed in Yvonne's artwork.*

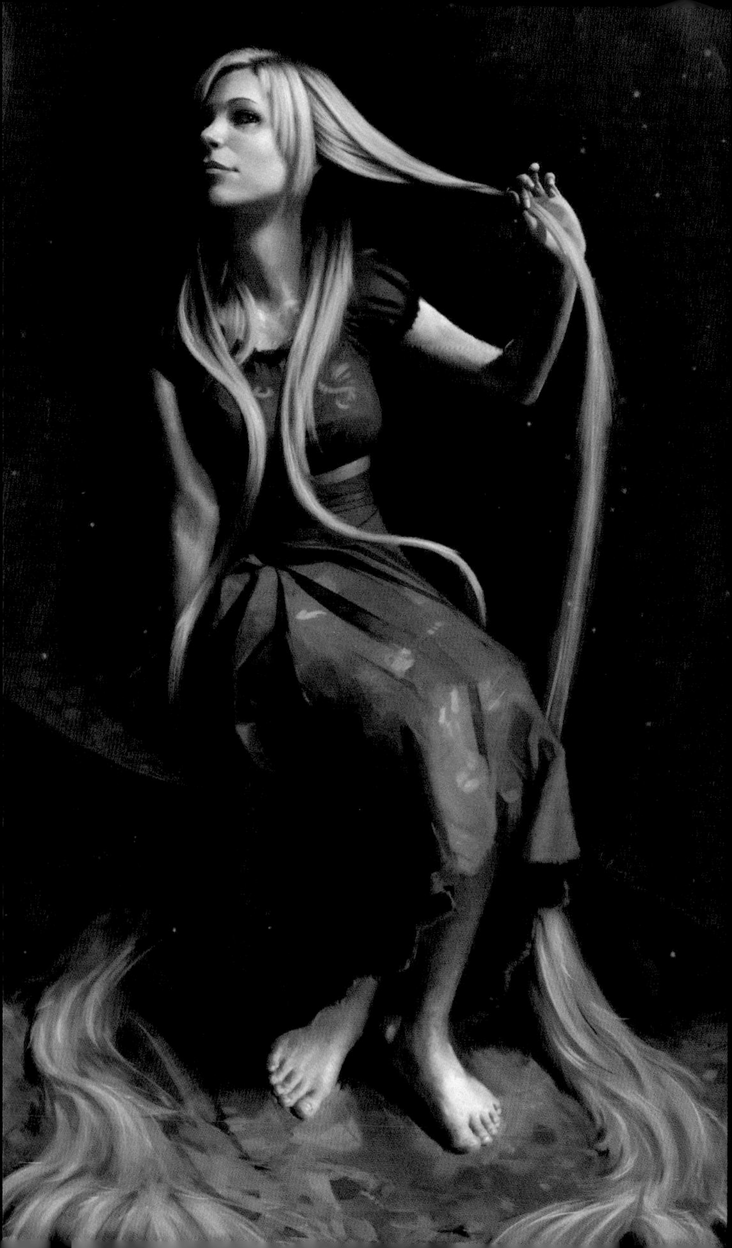

◄ **Rapunzel**
Bryan Beaux Beus
Portfolio work
Corel Painter
www.beauxpaint.com

"Rapunzel, Rapunzel, let down your hair, so that I may climb the golden stair," is the famous line from this traditional German fairy tale, recorded by the Brothers Grimm. First published in 1812, as part of Children's and Household Tales, *its plot has been widely referenced and parodied in popular culture ever since, and has been illustrated in many styles throughout countless collections of fairy stories. Bryan's portrayal shows Rapunzel running her fingers through her golden tresses.*

▶ **Olive Skinned in Cobalt Fur**
Jim Pavelec
Magazine cover
Heavy Metal magazine
Oil on paper and Adobe Photoshop
www.jimpavelec.com

This piece was created for
Heavy Metal *magazine, and
for Jim it was a particularly
memorable commission. "I got
the opportunity to meet one of
my earliest artistic influences,
Kevin Eastman, who is editor-in-
chief of* Heavy Metal. *He asked
me to do the piece for him,
which was a special honor for
me. I started the painting in oil
on paper, but then moved into
Photoshop to finish the piece."*

CHAPTER 5

◄ **Awakening Maro**
Anthony S. Waters
Collectible card game
illustration
Future Sight from
Wizards of the Coast
Adobe Photoshop
www.thinktankstudios.com

*Anthony's brief was to create
a magical incarnation of
nature: "The Maro is waking
up from a long, apocalypse-
induced slumber. How you
use light goes a long way
toward defining emotional
content. The same is true of
color. I used strong, high-key
greens on his face to suggest
this rise from hibernation."*

▶ **Sorcerer**
Emily Hare
Portfolio work
Colored pencil and
Adobe Photoshop

For this portrait, Emily used one of her neighbors as inspiration and reference. "He had a 'twinkle in the eye' that was ideal for an old wizard! I did most of the painting in Photoshop, incorporating textures here and there to add character, and took photos of burning incense for reference when painting the smoke. I wanted to give the impression of a magician who had been a bit of a rascal in his day, now enjoying a quiet pipe between incantations."

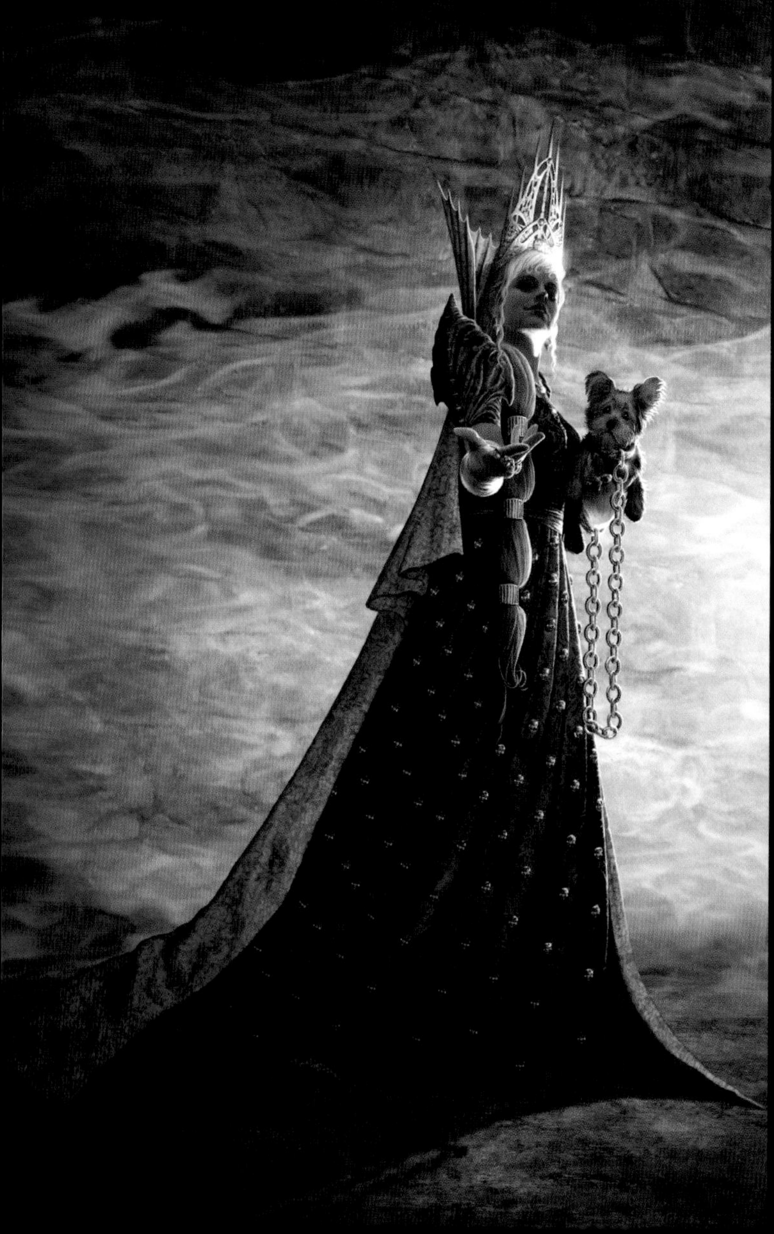

◄ **Blue Queen**
Martin McKenna
Book cover
The Key to Rondo from
Scholastic/Omnibus Books
Adobe Photoshop
www.martinmckenna.net

*This image, a detail from a
much larger digital canvas,
was delivered to the client in
fully editable layers. This was
to enable the cover design to
introduce graphical elements
between the layers, meaning
that the book's logo, for
example, could be positioned
behind the figure. As a result,
this isn't quite a fully realized
composition. Only the figure of
the queen, holding her captive
pet, has been rendered in detail.*

▶ **The Pig Walker**
David M. Bowers
Portfolio work
Oil on wood
www.dmbowers.com

Reminiscent of work from the 18th century portrait and landscape painter, Thomas Gainsborough, this surreal vision contains a sobering undertone. David reveals, "Urban populations are more divorced from their food supplies than ever before. There is total ignorance of how farmers raise the food that magically appears wrapped in plastic, canned, or frozen in our local grocery stores. As long as the Thanksgiving turkey appears on time, nobody thinks about how vulnerable we all are if something breaks the chain of supply."

◄ **Mystica**
Felipe Machado Franco
Album cover
Axel Rudi Pell from SPV
Adobe Photoshop
http://finalfrontier.thunderblast.net

This recording artist was very specific about the visuals to be created for his album cover, as Felipe recalls: "Axel Rudi Pell sent me a simple line drawing he'd made showing all the elements and basic composition. I began work on the background of mountains. I then made the skull towers, cave, and boat. I worked in detail on each figure in separate files, for which I photographed myself in different poses wearing a cloak."

▼ **Merlin**
Yvonne Gilbert
Portfolio work
Colored pencil
www.yvonnegilbert.com

*Wizards have appeared in myths, folktales, and
literature throughout recorded history. Magicians are
common characters in works of fantasy literature and
role-playing games, drawn from figures in mythology
and folklore — perhaps none more so than Merlin the
magician, the wizard featured in Arthurian legend.
Born the son of an incubus and mortal woman, Merlin
inherited his powers from his strange birth, but here
Yvonne has depicted him deep in arcane study.*

Methuselah

◄ **Methuselah (Gift of Tongues)**
Rick Sardinha
Portfolio work
Oil on masonite
www.battleduck.com

This is a painting that was inspired, explains Rick, by the Redwall *books of Brian Jacques. "I really love the books because they combine my love for wildlife with fantasy, on a really fun level. The central figure of this work is Methuselah, an ancient mouse at Redwall Abbey, a sort of patriarch and recorder of events. He is the only mouse with the gift of tongues, meaning he can talk to any other creature, though he stops at snakes and doesn't like foxes."*

▶ **Garga's Concern**
Matt Gaser
Adobe Photoshop and
Ambient Design ArtRage
www.mattgaser.com

*This whimsical image provides
us with a snapshot of the surreal
hustle and bustle of a bizarrely
cosmopolitan city of the
imagination. "In this painting,
I wanted to show an everyday
scene in a fantasy world where
strange beings, large and small,
live together with humans. In
my personal work, I strive to
create images of wild invention
that capture a moment as if you
are seeing a still from a film."*

◀ **A Fool's Love (Alas)**
Karen Ann Hollingsworth
Portfolio work
Watercolor and pencil on canvas
www.wrenditions.com

*Karen was inspired by a
deliberate triple misquote from
Shakespeare's* Hamlet: *"A lass,
poor Yorick! She knew him
well." Karen explains, "The
lady's bedchamber alludes
to their relationship; the hat
and the painting's title refer
to Yorick as court jester. The
decoration on the skull was
influenced by an ossuary in
which women's skulls were
painted with flowers and men's
with laurel or ivy, a motif I
incorporated into the border."*

▶ **Mialee Prepares Her Spells**
Ralph Horsley
Book illustration
Shattered Gates of Slaughtergarde
from Wizards of the Coast
Acrylic
www.ralphhorsley.co.uk

*An elf studies a spell book in
an abandoned library, while
goblins creep up behind her.
"I wanted to convey the magical
nature of the book and make
Mialee the focus, so I chose a
contrasting color scheme. The
yellow appears bold against the
blue-purple, and uses the lightest
values. After this initial impact,
the viewer's eye will then
wander into the background
to pick out the goblins. This
hopefully achieves a balance
between impact, and reward
for closer attention."*

◀ **Angel of Death**
Abrar Ajmal
T-shirt and poster for
Skulbone USA
Adobe Photoshop
www.aaillustrations.com

*Abrar explains that inspiration
for this powerful figure came to
him when he was working for
a miniatures company that, at
the time, were producing a game
about angels. "As luck would have
it, I soon had the opportunity to
develop the concept when I was
commissioned to produce
artwork with a strongly gothic
theme. The idea was to represent
the figure of Death with a slight
twist. What if, for some people,
he is a symbol of salvation rather
than just one of dread?"*

▶ **Death and the Serpent of Caol**
Kieran Yanner
Portfolio work
Adobe Photoshop
www.kieranyanner.com

*Much of Kieran's work
utilizes a technique similar
to that of matte painting:
using photographs in collage
or montage, then combining
this with digital paint, and
sometimes acrylic or oil. "I
adopted this fast technique to
meet ever-tightening deadlines,
and I stuck with it because it
achieved the look that I wanted.
This piece relied much more on
painting than photomontage.
I'd always wanted to paint a
mysterious cloaked figure,
and this is my realization
of that desire."*

◄ **The Tongues of Fire**
Sam Araya
Game illustration for
White Wolf Publishing
Adobe Photoshop
http://paintagram.blogspot.com

*Achieving a balance, or
complete dissonance, between
abstract forms and the human
figure is something that has
always interested Sam, he says.
"The same can be said about the
interaction between painting
and elements of photomontage.
This piece represents a small
step toward what I want to
achieve in my future work;
the integration of my formal
study of graphic design with
my self-taught approach
to illustration."*

◀ **Little People Parliament**
Eric Scala
Book illustration
Little Big from Terre de Brume
Adobe Photoshop and
Corel Painter
www.ericscala.com

*In Eric's picture we spy upon
fairy folk in a modern city
park at night. "The idea was
to create a scene depicting
a parliament for the little
people. The good are lit
in the brighter area of the
group, while in the dark
are the more mischievous.
My intention was to give
the image the look of a
traditional painting."*

◀ **Zephyr's Tomb**
William O'Connor
Portfolio work
Adobe Photoshop
www.wocstudios.com

*A composition intended
to illustrate movement, the
sweeping design is accentuated
by the blowing leaves and
armor detailing. "When I am
composing images, I constantly
try to simplify my designs.
Although there is a great deal
of detail, the overall design is
very simple. Texture is the
concentration of this piece."*

▶ **Peter Pan in Scarlet**
Tony DiTerlizzi
Book cover
Peter Pan in Scarlet from
Margaret K. McElderry
Gouache on board
www.diterlizzi.com

*This re-imagining of a classic
character was understandably a
tough challenge for Tony. "Many
people have preconceived ideas
of how certain literary heroes
should appear. The trick here
was to design the character
in a way that acknowledges
what has come before, while
at the same time pushing the
character's design forward
for a new audience."*

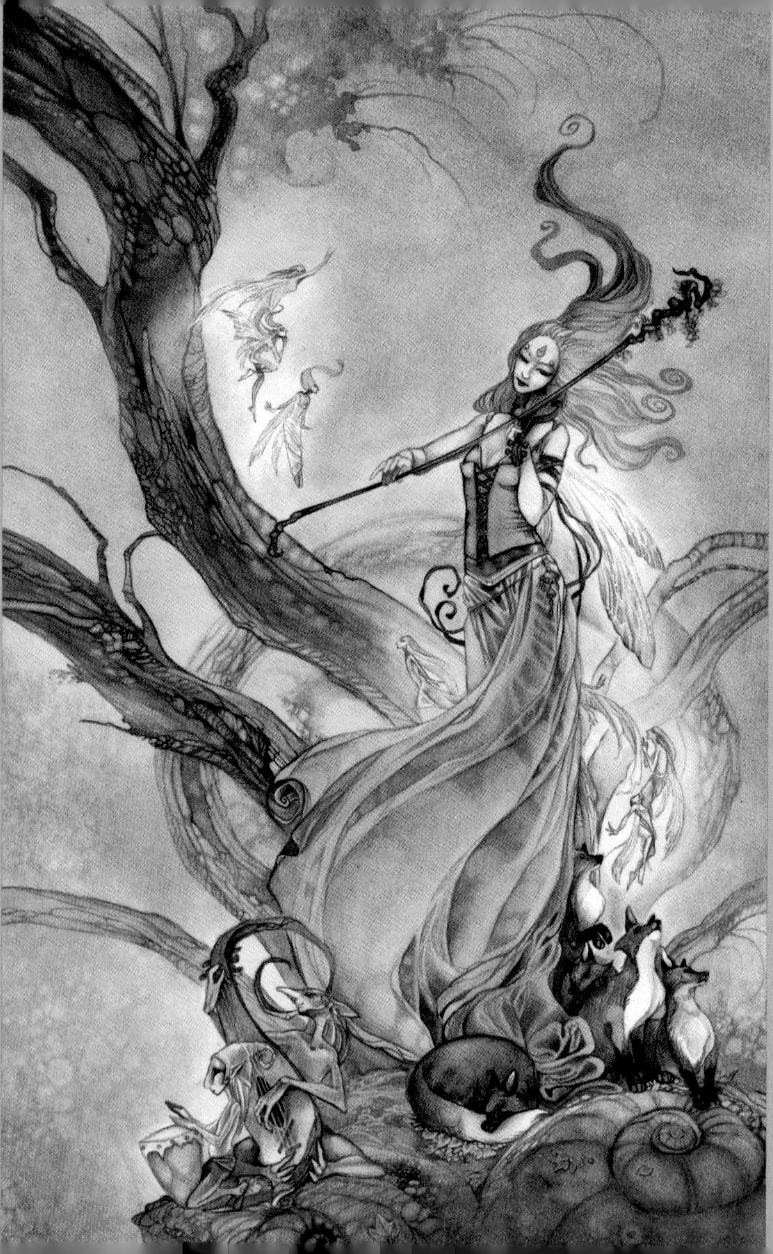

◄ **Page of Wands**
Stephanie Law
Portfolio work
Watercolor
www.shadowscapes.com

This delicate watercolor painting forms part of Stephanie's Shadowscapes Tarot series, about which she tells us more: "The Page of Wands is the embodiment of passion, confidence, and creative potential; a being who is assured and assertive. She is also a messenger, conveying, as I like to think, Henry Wadsworth Longfellow's sentiment that music is the universal language."

► **The Enchanting**
Nick Harris
Portfolio work
Corel Painter and
Autodesk Sketchbook Pro

Nick is heavily inspired by the style of Victorian painters and the Pre-Raphaelites. "I come from a traditional art background, and treat digital art in the same way. After importing this drawing from Sketchbook Pro, I added a base color, and worked into it with the oil pastel variant to establish some tonal values. This gave me something to place washes of color over to bring to life the lights and darks."

▶ **Imagine**
Karen Ann Hollingsworth
Portfolio work
Watercolor and pencil
www.wrenditions.com

Two distinct methods were used while working on this picture, as Karen reveals: "One style is very controlled, composing a tight pencil drawing using reference. The second approach I use is extremely spontaneous, finding shapes within a watercolor wash using colored pencils. It's very meditative, like imagining shapes in clouds. The sweeping dove form suddenly emerged while using this second technique."

◄ **Old World Leprechaun**
Tony DiTerlizzi
Book illustration
*Arthur Spiderwick's Field Guide to
the Fantastical World Around You*
from Simon & Schuster
Gouache on board
www.diterlizzi.com

*This is one of Tony's favorites
of the thirty-plus plates he
produced for the centerpiece of
The Spiderwick Chronicles
books. "I like it because it
captures a lot of philosophy
behind the series; to take
traditional, classic, and trite
fantasy characters, and reinvent
them through character design.
This piece pays homage to not
only my fantasy influences, like
Arthur Rackham and Brian
Froud, but to classic illustrators
like Norman Rockwell."*

▶ **Goddess of Industry**
Jian Guo
Magazine illustration
The Magazine from Sci-Fi World
Corel Painter
http://breathing2004.gfxartist.com

At first glance, this Arcadian figure appears to have only organic flowing forms echoing nature, whereas in fact, Jian has portrayed the physical embodiment of technology and industry. The circuitry-laced fiery glow within the character's leaf-like collar and cuff are representative of the blast furnaces of a steel mill, while details of her costume suggest roller chains and other mechanisms. Most symbolic of all is the gear wheel hovering in her grasp.

◀ **A Fascinating Bloom**
Soa Lee
Promotional image for
Legend Footwear
Autodesk 3ds Max and
Adobe Photoshop
www.soanala.com

*Soa Lee's glossy characterization
of this glamorous, modern fairy
was designed to appear in an
advertisement for women's
shoes. "It's a spring morning,
and Christina the fairy, who
fell asleep in a garden of red
flowers, has been woken by
dawn's sunlight. She unfolds
her wings with a beautiful whirl
of color, while red petals open
wide and sparkling pollen
starts to dance."*

▶ **Daniel**
Kieran Yanner
Portfolio work
Adobe Photoshop and
Corel Painter
www.kieranyanner.com

*This painting was developed by
Kieran from a series of sketches,
and finally brought to fully
rendered fruition. "Originally,
the composition had a crowd
of upward reaching arms in
worship of this fallen angel.
I later made changes to this
when a client requested printing
rights to the piece, but wanted
it in a slightly different context
and format. I agreed and
altered the piece as seen here,
but the original version can still
be viewed on my website."*

◀ **Lovecats**
Benita Winkler
Portfolio work
Adobe Photoshop
http://eeanee.com

Benita has shown this
enchanting fairy witch sitting
beneath a weeping willow
tree, as she uses her magical
powers to conjure delicate feline
companions out of the tree's
catkins. Catkins, or aments,
are slim, cylindrical flower
clusters without petals. Many
other trees, including oak,
birch, hazel, and chestnut, also
bear catkins, which, in ancient
folklore, are said to contain
magical properties.

▶ **Angelic Corruption**
Kevin Crossley
Portfolio work
Adobe Photoshop
www.kevcrossley.com

Here, Kevin depicts a once celestial character, now dissolute; her skewered arms alluding to her newly found deviancy. "This picture is my first foray into the world of clichéd female fantasy figures. Surprisingly, hardly anyone notices her pierced arms. Photos of ferns and trees were incorporated into the background, using filters and blending modes. I made extensive use of Photoshop's Brush tool as well as the Dodge, Sponge, and Burn tools."

◄ **Little One**
Roberto Campus
Album cover
LuxaAeterna by Aquaria
Oils and Adobe Photoshop
www.robertocampus.com

*This is one of the pieces that
Roberto is most proud of, and
it originally took him only three
hours to put together. "There
was an art contest and I didn't
have anything to submit, so
one evening I rushed to my
desk and, after rummaging
through the fairy-inspired photo
references I have of my daughter
Gwendolyn, the concept came
to mind. The final image was
ready in the blink of an eye. I
didn't win the contest, but this
slightly revised version of the
image was later used as an
album cover."*

► **Skimming the Surface**
Stephanie Law
Portfolio work
Watercolor
www.shadowscapes.com

*The unicorn is a legendary
creature, whose power is
exceeded only by its mystery.
Though the modern popular
image of the unicorn is that of
a horse, the traditional unicorn
has a billy-goat beard, a lion's
tail, and an antelope's cloven
hooves. Stephanie has shown her
unicorn magically cantering
lightly across ocean waves.
"Unicorns are said to have
been born from the sea. They
are creatures of light, air, and
sea foam, and they are wild as
the ocean."*

◀ **Rose River**
Marcel Baumann
Portfolio work
Adobe Photoshop

Developed from the rough sketch of a fantasy forest, Marcel enjoyed the process of painting without a clear concept in mind, his only plan being to create a romantic scene. Each stage of the composition developed organically; the design, shapes, and lighting being rendered instinctively. "It was easy to alter the mood in Photoshop very quickly by changing the colors and brightness, which each time took the work in a new direction."

▶ **Faydrums**
Benita Winkler
Portfolio work
Adobe Photoshop
http://eeanee.com

In Benita's crepuscular green swamp, a fairy creature delicately cups her ear to listen, perhaps for sounds of slumber. The signs are that she inhabits the realm of sleep and dreams, as the plant she holds in her other hand is an opium poppy, a symbol of Morpheus. In Greek mythology, Morpheus is the principal god who shapes our dreams, and from him the drug morphine derives its name, based on its dream-inducing power.

◀ **Garden of Giants**
Michael Zancan
Portfolio work
Autodesk 3ds Max
and Adobe Photoshop
http://zancan.fr

*The scene in this painting
presents a metaphor for that
intense and rare feeling of
crying for joy, Michael explains:
"Creating this has been like
going on a long, epic adventure.
Several preliminary studies of
the main characters were drawn
on paper. The building, inspired
by Art Nouveau architecture, such
as the Grand Palais in Paris,
was designed and rendered in
3D. This gave me a reliable
perspective base for the initial
drawing, onto which I painted
the scene digitally."*

CHAPTER 7
SCENES AND SETTINGS

◀ **Spring Sunset**
Andreas Rocha
Portfolio work
Autodesk 3ds Max and
Adobe Photoshop
www.andreasrocha.com

"*This took me three days,
starting with a couple of
sketches. I created a basic
model in 3ds Max with some
textures applied, which
I brought into Photoshop.
I painted over the 3D render,
incorporating a lot of
photographic elements. I've
always had a fascination for
sweeping, fantasy landscapes
that immerse the viewer and
engage the imagination.*"

▶ **Chinese Winter**
Raphael Lacoste
Portfolio work
Adobe Photoshop
www.raphael-lacoste.com

*Having a strong background in
3D graphics, Raphael explains
that he wanted to paint something
entirely in 2D for practice.
"I painted this during the winter,
when I was inspired by the cold
Canadian climate. I enjoyed the
perspective, working on the
foggy houses and roofs to make
everything organic, rather than
straight and obvious. The pencil
is better than 3D software to create
this kind of composition. There is
a subtle steampunk mood to it,
with factory structures just visible
in the distance."*

◄ **The Journey**
Michael See
Portfolio work
Adobe Photoshop
*http://michaelzhsee.cgsociety.
org/gallery*

*Michael depicts a festival
of lights, behind which lies
his cautionary tale. "The
inhabitants of this world
remember the earth through
stories of a once beautiful place.
Environmental disaster caused
by man meant that the earth
could no longer sustain life.
The human race prolonged its
existence by traveling to harsh
planets on which colonists make
desperate attempts to fashion
lives like those remembered
from home. Although the earth
is dead to them, people pay
homage to her by offering up
to the heavens these lanterns of
light, hope, and mourning."*

▶ **Locke Lamora**
Benjamin Carre
Book cover
*Les Mensonges de Locke
Lamora* from Bragelonne
Adobe Photoshop
www.blancfonce.com

*In this image, we journey into an
extravagant city; a shimmering
and exaggerated alternative
Venice. We observe the complexity
of its maze-like architecture, in
the company of the somewhat
piratical figure standing on the
quayside. But we're also allowed
to dive into the deep, murky
waters. Benjamin split the
composition into a cross-section,
enabling us to catch a glimpse
of the extraordinary, submerged
metallic infrastructure supporting
the ancient streets, houses, and
bridges towering above.*

◄ **Ravnica Mountains**
Anthony S. Waters
Collectible card game illustration
Ravnica from Wizards of the Coast
Adobe Photoshop and
Corel Painter
www.thinktankstudios.com

*Anthony produced a total
of five large environment
paintings for the* Magic:
The Gathering, Ravnica
*project. "This piece, showing
the gigantic growth of factories
that form the mountains on this
world, was by far the hardest to
complete. It remains one of the
most densely detailed pieces
I've ever created."*

► **The Broken Orrery**
Paul Bourne
Portfolio work
Daz Bryce and Corel Paint Shop Pro
www.contestedground.co.uk

*A heliocentric device, showing
the relative positions and motions
of heavenly bodies, this orrery
illustrates an unknown solar
system. As Paul describes,
"I always liked the idea of
ancient civilizations and archaic
technology, the purpose of which
having been long since forgotten.
That's what this image presents:
an ancient orrery built by some
long-dead civilization, rusting
and undiscovered, its secrets
soon to be lost forever."*

► **Water Valley**
Marcel Baumann
Portfolio work
Adobe Photoshop

"Beautiful plants, their shapes, and how they looked in sunlight, inspired me to try creating a calm and dreamlike natural environment. I decided to use a verdant valley, with waterfalls as my main theme, creating a natural amphitheatre, and suggesting how the water had formed this place over time."

►► **Pirates**
Patrick Reilly
Portfolio work
Adobe Photoshop and Corel Painter
http://preilly.deviantart.com/gallery

A delightfully crepuscular seascape, which recalls the spectral green-tinged paintings of the Victorian artist John Atkinson Grimshaw. Patrick elaborates, "I've been a longtime fan of popular folklore, whether it's sea monsters, gremlins, or, in this case, tales of ghost ships sailing the high seas. This depicts an old ghost ship returning to port, long after it was thought to have been lost at sea."

▲ **Home**
Andreas Rocha
Portfolio work
Adobe Photoshop and Corel Painter
www.andreasrocha.com

For this painting, Andreas was inspired by the Torre de Belém, a major landmark in Lisbon. He has captured a monochromatic air of solitude; cold, but with the glowing fire providing a warm focal point. "I've always loved rainy coastal environments. This took me about a day to complete in Photoshop, with a lot of help from Painter, to achieve those 'wet and rainy' brush strokes of the green-gray colors that are so characteristic of heavy thunderstorms."

▲ **Gluba Vanderhon the Giant**
Matt Gaser
Portfolio work
Adobe Photoshop
www.mattgaser.com

A panorama that's delightfully playful in its use of scale, this is a scene set at what first appears to be a fairly intimate level, but which soon reveals layers of worlds within worlds, containing many miniature tableaux. "In this painting, I wanted to show a wide shot of a grand fantastical moment like nothing anyone has seen before. Once I finished the piece, it spawned an entire personal project that I've continued to develop into a storyline."

◀ **Ravnica Plains**
Anthony S. Waters
Collectible card game illustration
Ravnica from Wizards of the Coast
Adobe Photoshop and Corel Painter
www.thinktankstudios.com

The work of famed French
comic artist, Moebius, was very
much on Anthony's mind as
he designed the Ravnica city
structures. He reveals more
about their concept: "Most of
the people of Ravnica live far
below the surface levels. Those
who rule the world get to cavort
at the very top. These elite
are the only ones to regularly
experience undiluted sunlight,
and they make the most of it,
channeling and containing it
within gigantic crystals."

◀ **Path to the Gothic Choir**
Raphael Lacoste
Portfolio work
Autodesk 3ds Max and
Adobe Photoshop
www.raphael-lacoste.com

*Raphael was inspired by
Caspar David Friedrich's
painting* Abbey in an Oak
Forest *for this picture. "I'm
quite a romantic artist and
I love 19th century paintings.
Between realism and stylization
lies a fascinating way of
depicting reality that's very
dramatic and theatrical. I love
to work on atmosphere and
moods, and here I hope you can
smell the smoke and feel the
mist of a humid early morning.
I created very simple shapes in
3ds Max, which I then painted
over in 2D."*

▶ **Cannot Prevent**
Ryohei Hase
Portfolio work
Adobe Photoshop
http://ryoheihase.com

*Amid this miserable crowd of
hunched figures, shambling
under their umbrellas through
a downpour, one woman
stands, detached and upright,
her entire head alight in a
sudden spectacular blaze. This
incendiary motif in Ryohei's
symbolic image represents
ignited anger and passions
bursting free from within this
frustrated proletarian, no
longer able to countenance
the bleak thronging procession
of her dreary, city commute.*

▲ **Empty Vessels**
Tony Hayes
Portfolio work
Adobe Photoshop, e frontier Poser, and E-on Vue d'Esprit
www.my-art-gallery.co.uk

Clive Barker's film Lord of Illusions *provided Tony with the inspiration for this image. "My intention was to create a stark, barren desert, littered with gaunt empty heads: a hellish place. I adjusted the lighting to give long, dark shadows, and black mouths and eyes, which reinforce the impression of the heads' emptiness. This is one of the few images that turned out exactly as I had envisaged, showing how simple ideas can be effective."*

► **Lancelot's Secret**
John Garner
Portfolio work
Oils and acrylic
www.shadowsofthunder.com

*John drew upon his love
of Arthurian legend as the
inspiration for this piece. "It
was created with many layers
of acrylic paint as a base. An
airbrush was used to add the
highlights and atmospheric
effects. Once the acrylic paint
was dry, oil washes were used to
deepen and enhance the colors.
No digital effects were used in
the creation of the painting."*

▼ **Ravnica Forest**
Anthony S. Waters
Collectible card game illustration
Ravnica from Wizards of the Coast
www.thinktankstudios.com

Anthony developed the environment for this card-based fantasy game. "I got to participate in all aspects of production on Ravnica, and illustrated its gigantic city. Certain parts of the city are dedicated to hydroponics, which are shown in this painting. This piece was a true pleasure to do, in every respect. I wanted to suggest a simultaneously artificial and organic space; the architecture reflecting the shapes of the trees that they are designed to shelter."

▶ **Goondabar Discovery**
Matt Gaser
Portfolio work
Ambient Design ArtRage and Adobe Photoshop
www.mattgaser.com

Here, we enter a landscape dominated by mysterious constructions of colossal size. Matt explains further: "Scale is a theme I've noticed creeping into my work a lot over the years. Perhaps it's the epic nature of the subject matter that attracts me. For this painting, I wanted to tell the story of a traveler who finds a robot leaving its post and walking, after being locked in stone for thousands of years. What happens next, I leave up to the viewer."

◀ **The Battle of Four Armies**
Jason Engle
Promotional image for
a miniatures company
Adobe Photoshop
www.jaestudio.com

*For Jason, this was one of
his most complex works.
Designed to show as many
characters as possible, it was
printed as a ten-foot-long
banner. Jason worked on a
digital canvas more than
four feet wide. He rendered
each character separately,
before placing them into
the main image, and then
painted the lighting and
environmental effects.*

◄ **Arcana Evolved**
J. P. Targete
Game book cover and novel cover
Arcana Evolved from Malhavoc Press
Adobe Photoshop
www.targeteart.com

To begin this piece, J. P. created
a detailed drawing, but this had
its drawbacks, as he explains:
"The under-drawing made the
painting very easy. The snag
was that it couldn't evolve much
because I'd shown it to my client
for approval. I still enjoyed
working on it and I wanted to
express a sense of epic drama
unfolding before the viewer. The
letterbox format lends itself to
such epic scenes. Composition,
along with form and light, are
controlled to enhance drama
and action."

► **Untitled**
Ryohei Hase
Portfolio work
Adobe Photoshop
http://ryoheihase.com

In this dark fantasy painting,
Ryohei shows a young sword-
wielding Japanese warrior
surrounded by towering,
lycanthrope horrors. The artist
captures the moment just before
his boy hero, already slashed
and bloody, begins his desperate
battle in earnest. Werewolves
and shape-shifters are common
in folk tales from all over the
world, and Japanese folklore
features many creatures that
are part-animal and part-
human, including the capricious
fox creatures, Kitsune.

◀ **Meatman vs. Werebear**
Michal Ivan
Game book cover
Adobe Photoshop
http://perzo.cgsociety.org/about

For this Czech role-playing game cover, Michal has depicted two of the monsters that are featured in the book; here seen locked in brutal combat. "Meatman is a monster inspired by the Frankenstein creature; its muscular form sewn together from dead tissue, and brought to life by magicians, while the grizzly Werebear is a bloodthirsty half-man, half-bear lycanthrope."

▶ **Zaramoth Unleased**
R. K. Post
Comic book cover for Dark Horse
Based on the video game *Dungeon Siege 2* from Gas Powered Games
Adobe Photoshop
www.rkpost.net

This titanic, multi-limbed, armored demon, engaged in bloody battle, was inspired by the Dungeon Siege *game world. But R. K. was under a lot of pressure to create the piece within a very tight production schedule, as he explains: "I didn't have much time to complete this one because it was done while I was working as an in-game artist for Gas Powered Games, and I was asked to produce this additional promotional painting."*

◀ **Dragon's Nest**
Anne Stokes
T-shirt design for Spiral Direct Ltd
Adobe Photoshop
www.annestokes.com

Anne needed to produce
artwork that was mostly light
against dark, to look good when
printed on black T-shirts. "The
foreshortening on the figure's
pose, and the diagonal line
between the dragon, the fire,
and the warrior, are intended to
heighten the sense of drama and
action. This mother dragon will
viciously guard her nest of eggs,
and the adventurer is in for a
lot of trouble."

◄ **Friday the 13th, October 1307**
Cyril Van Der Haegen
Portfolio work
Adobe Photoshop and
Corel Painter
www.tegehel.org

*On this fateful night in France,
hundreds of Knights Templar
were arrested by agents of Philip
IV, and later tortured into
admitting heresy. Cyril explains,
"These poor fellows are escaping
through a secret passage, while
the militia pounds on the door
upstairs. They're frantically
hiding a chest, which might even
contain the Holy Grail." What
became of the great Templar
treasures in France has long
been a mystery.*

► **Kicking Back**
Ralph Horsley
Book illustration
Cityscapes from Wizards
of the Coast
Acrylic
www.ralphhorsley.co.uk

*Ralph was asked to compose
a busy tavern scene containing
several key elements. "One of the
hardest aspects was that the two
key characters, a halfling and a
gnome, were also physically the
smallest. I tackled this challenge
by placing them above the
action. This enabled a good
overview of the bar scene, and
the ability to make them a lot
larger within the perspective.
The other incidents were then
subtly picked out with brighter
lighting, as if sunlight were
coming in through a window."*

◀ **The Dragon Wrangler**
Nick Harris
Portfolio work
Adobe Photoshop and Corel Painter

*Nick describes how the complex
textures on this dragon are
simply a result of playing
with the large chalk variant
in Painter, combined with
a variety of paper surfaces.
"You can adjust the scale of
paper, invert it, and even
control how much grain a tool
picks up, so there's wonderful
potential, even within this
one combination. If you add
experimental mark-making
over the top to help define the
contours of the form, it really
does become a powerful tool."*

▶ **Serra Angel vs Spectre**
Greg Staples
Collectible card game illustration
Magic: The Gathering
from Wizards of the Coast
Corel Painter
www.gregstaples.co.uk

*Greg has long been inspired
by classic fantasy imagery, and
like many other leading artists
working today, it was the heroic
fantasy paintings of Frank
Frazetta that first captured
his young imagination.
"Frightening, and epic, these
are the things that drive me
today; needless to say, the
images have never left me."*

▶ **Garhunt**
Karl Richardson
Collectible card game illustration
World of Warcraft from Upper Deck
Adobe Photoshop
www.epilogue.net/cgi/database/
art/list.pl?gallery=14213

*Karl's brief was to portray
an Orc Warlock, flanked by
his guard. "When illustrating
for cards, I usually fill the
composition with a close-up.
It's generally a subconscious
decision because I enjoy painting
facial detail, which can be lost
when the art is printed so
small. With this image, I had
to pull back and show more of
the figures, because the demon
guard is such a big character."*

◀ **Werewolf the Pure**
Abrar Ajmal
Game book cover
Werewolf: the Pure from
White Wolf Publishing
Adobe Photoshop
www.aaillustrations.com

*A pack of cruelly rapacious
lycanthropes destroy all in
their path in Abrar's aggressive
vision. "I approached this image
with the desire to dramatically
illustrate rage, and also to
produce as eye-catching a cover
for the book as I could. I wanted
the piece to tell a story. The
burning buildings in the
background indicate events
leading up to this moment,
and give us an idea of what
these guys are capable of."*

▶ **The Battle of Agincourt:**
25 October 1415
Donato Giancola
Book cover
The Crippled Angel from Tor Books
Oil on paper on panel
www.donatoarts.com

*In this powerful painting,
Donato didn't want to capture
the heroics of battle, but rather
show the great equalizing force
that conflict has upon those
engaged in face-to-face mortal
combat. As he says, "Nobleman,
mercenary, and peasant share
a common fate upon the
battlefield, especially during
a conflict such as Agincourt.
There are no true winners."*

ADEL ADILI
www.adel3d.com
adel3d@yahoo.com
Daphne & Apollo *p111*
Rostam *p52–53*

ABRAR AJMAL
www.aaillustrations.com
abrar.ajmal@ntlworld.com
Angel of Death *p214*
Pirates *p11*
Werewolf the Pure *p185*

JULIA ALEKSEEVA
http://julax.ru
email@cg-warrior.com
Dragon's World *p146–147*
Guenhwyvar *p4, p103*

JEFF ANDERSON
jeffand145@aol.com
Riddler's Fayre 2 *p35*

GLEN ANGUS
Odin *p12–13*
Thor, Ultimate *p132–133*

SAM ARAYA
http://paintagram.
blogspot.com
paintagram@gmail.com
The Tongues of Fire *p218*
© White Wolf Publishing

MARCEL BAUMANN
marcelbaumann@gmx.ch
Rose River *p248–249, p318–319*
Water Valley *p266–267*

BRYAN BEAUX BEUS
www.beauxpaint.com
untitleduser@gmail.com
Honey Queen *p154*
Rapunzel *p190*

KEREM BEYIT
http://kerembeyit.gfxartist.com
www.theartofkerembeyit.com
kerembeyit@hotmail.com
Claw Clan *p157*
White Tiger Clan *p38–39*

PASCAL BLANCHE
www.3dluvr.com/pascalb
lobo971@yahoo.com
Hunters *p37*

PAUL BOURNE
www.contestedground.co.uk
paul@contestedground.co.uk
The Broken Orrery *p265*
"Thou Shall Not Pass!" *p14*

DAVID M. BOWERS
www.dmbowers.com
davidmbowers@comcast.net
The Pig Walker *p201*

MATTHEW BRADBURY
www.epilogue.net/cgi/data-
base/art/list.pl?gallery=11601
mattbradbury2000@yahoo.com
Dragon Rider *p80–81*
The Last Days *p142–143*
The Watchmaker *p95*

SIMON DOMINIC BREWER
www.painterly.co.uk
simon@painterly.co.uk
Minotaur *p139*

CARLOS CABRERA
www.carloscabrera.com.ar
sayhi@carloscabrera.com.ar
Minotaur *p83*

ROBERTO CAMPUS
www.robertocampus.com
bob@robertocampus.com
Little One *p244*

BENJAMIN CARRE
www.blancfonce.com
benjamincarre@gmail.com
Locke Lamora *p261*
© Bragelonne
Prophecy *p145*
© Flammarion
Ulysse *p122*
© Père castor-Flammarion

ROBERT CHANG
www.ethereality.info
web@ethereality.info
Black Wolf Ronin *p22–23*
Scythe Wolf *p76*
Till Death Do Us Part *p40–41*

MIKE CORRIERO
www.mikecorriero.com
mikecorriero@gmail.com
Keeper of the Fields *p158*
Tiltadron *p150*

KEVIN CROSSLEY
www.kevcrossley.com
bombjak69@hotmail.com
Angelic Corruption *p243*
Krike Dragon *p121*

MELANIE DELON
www.melaniedelon.com
esk@eskarina-circus.com
What I See *p185*

SACHA "ANGEL" DIENER
www.angel3d.ch
angel@angel3d.ch
Flames of Magic *p181*
Spellsword *p79*

TONY DITERLIZZI
www.diterlizzi.com
Old World Leprechaun *p232*
Peter Pan in Scarlet *p224–225*

JASON ENGLE
www.jaestudio.com
jae@jaestudio.com
The Battle of Four Armies
p288–289
Dark Knight *p55*
Dreamfall *p68*
Knights of Ansalon *p17*

FELIPE MACHADO FRANCO
http://finalfrontier.
thunderblast.net
newdimensionart@yahoo.com
As Holy as They Come *p178*
Mystica *p202–203*
The Golden Armour *p21*

XIAO-CHEN FU
http://krishna-fu.cgsociety.org
krishna860@hotmail.com
Chi You and Taotie *p45*
Kill the Winter *p71*

DENISE GARNER
www.towerwindow.com
denise@towerwindow.com
Dragon Skins *p64*
Temptation *p108–109*

JOHN GARNER
www.shadowsofthunder.com
john@shadowsofthunder.com
Lancelot's Secret *p282–283*
Spawning Ground *p114–115*

MATT GASER
www.mattgaser.com
mgaser@mac.com
Garga's Concern *p208–209*
Gluba Vanderhon the Giant
p272–273
Goondabar Discovery *p286–287*

DONATO GIANCOLA
www.donatoarts.com
donato@donatoart.com
The Battle of Agincourt:
25 October 1415 *p312–313*

YVONNE GILBERT
www.yvonnegilbert.com
yvonne.gilbert@dsl.pipex.com
Ice Dragon *p104*
Lady of Shalott *p189*
Merlin *p204–205*

REBECCA GUAY
www.rebeccaguay.com
rebeccaguay@yahoo.com
Angel of First Love *p168*
© 2007 Rebecca Guay and
Angel Quest Inc
Beauty and the Unicorn *p125*
Cupid and Psyche *p107*
Mev *p182*
© 2007 Rebecca Guay and
D. Legro

JIAN GUO
http://breathing2004.gfxartist.
com
beathing2004@yahoo.com.cn
Bone of the Ocean *p60*
Goddess of Industry *p235*
The Last Guardian *p91*

EMILY HARE
emily.hare@gmail.com
Sorcerer *p197*

NICK HARRIS
(Virgil Pomfret Artists Agency)
virgil.pomfret@online.fr
Dragon Wrangler *p304*
The Enchanting *p228–229*
Siren Song *p170–171*

LEO HARTAS
www.hartas.eclipse.co.uk
leo@hartas.eclipse.co.uk
Mountain Dragons *p89*

RYOHEI HASE
http://ryoheihase.com
ryohei_hase@f6.dion.ne.jp
Cannot Prevent *p279*
Untitled *p293*

TONY HAYES
www.my-art-gallery.co.uk
tonyhayes@blueyonder.co.uk
Day Dreamer *p173*
Empty Vessels *p280–281*

KORY HEINZEN
kory@korysdiner.com
http://korysdiner.homestead.com
Hard Day's Work *p28–29*

RICHARD HESCOX
www.richardhescox.com
triffid@charter.net
Night *p166–167*

JON HODGSON
www.jonhodgson.com
jonnyhodgsonart@gmail.com
Shugenja *p72–73*
© Alderac Entertainment Group
Yobanjin Wyrm *p84–85*
© Alderac Entertainment Group

**KAREN ANN
HOLLINGSWORTH**
www.wrenditions.com
karen@wrenditions.com
A Fool's Love (Alas) *p210–211*
Imagine *p230–231*

KUANG HONG
www.zemotion.net
noah@zemotion.net
End of Godliness *p63*
The Disciplinant *p136*

RALPH HORSLEY
www.ralphhorsley.co.uk
email@ralphhorsley.co.uk
City of Peril *p129*
© Wizards of the Coast
Kicking Back *p303*
© Wizards of the Coast
Mialee Prepares Her Spells *p213*
© Wizards of the Coast
Realms of Sorcery *p96–97*
© Games Workshop

TONY HOUGH
www.tonyhough.co.uk
tonyhough2000@yahoo.co.uk
Byakhee *p92*

MICHAL IVAN
http://perzo.cgsociety.org/about
mivan@ba.psg.sk
Bogatyr *p46*
Jaga *p67*
Meatman vs. Werebear *p294*

UWE JARLING
www.jarling-arts.com
uwe@jarling-arts.com
Majestic Dignity *p167*
Mighty Dragon *p149*

CAMILLE KUO
http://camilkuo.com/main.htm
camilkuo@hotmail.com
Cerebrus *p153*
Dunhuang *p135*

RAPHAEL LACOSTE
www.raphael-lacoste.com
Raphael.lacoste@gmail.com
Chinese Winter *p257*
Path to the Gothic Choir
p276–277

CLINT LANGLEY
www.clintlangley.com
anjahemmerich@yahoo.com
Blood of the Dragon *p100*
Blood of the Dragon novel
cover, for the Black Library/
Games Workshop Limited
(www.blacklibrary.com).
Copyright Games Workshop
Ltd 2005. Used with permission.
Slaine *p26*
Slaine © Copyright 2007
Rebellion A/S. All rights reserved.
www.2000ADonline.com

STEPHANIE LAW
www.shadowscapes.com
stephlaw@gmail.com
Page of Wands *p226*
Skimming the Surface
p246–247

SOA LEE
www.soanala.com
soanala@naver.com
A Fascinating Bloom *p236*

DARYL MANDRYK
www.mandrykart.com
blackarts@shaw.ca
Silver *p32*
Stalker *p2*

MARTIN MCKENNA
www.martinmckenna.net
martin@martinmckenna.net
Blue Queen *p198*
Eye of the Dragon *p117*
Spell Breaker *p131*
Temple of Terror *p99*

WILLIAM O'CONNOR
www.wocstudios.com
woconnor@wocstudios.com
Fire and Water *p25*
Zephyr's Tomb *p222–223*

JIM PAVELEC
www.jimpavelec.com
Genethoq@comcast.net
Olive Skinned in Cobalt Fur *p193*
Wererats *p161*

R. K. POST
www.rkpost.net
postrk@aol.com
Benrig Medb *p186–187*
Eva in Repose *p56–57*
Zaramoth Unleashed *p297*

PATRICK REILLY
http://preilly.deviantart.com/
gallery
reilly1138@msn.com
Pirates *p268–269*
Tales from the High Seas
p140–141
Wrecking Crew *p162*

KARL RICHARDSON
www.epilogue.net/cgi/database/
art/list.pl?gallery=14213
karl.richardson24@ntlworld.com
Garhunt *p308–309*
© 2007 The Upper Deck
Company; World of Warcraft
© 2004–2007 Blizzard
Entertainment, Inc.
Ulk Rider *p50*

ANDREAS ROCHA
www.andreasrocha.com
rocha.andreas@gmail.com
Home *p270–271*
Spring Sunset *p4–5, p254–255*

RICK SARDINHA
www.battleduck.com
rick@battleduck.com
Elemental Moon *p126*
Methuselah (Gift of Tongues)
p206

ERIC SCALA
www.ericscala.com
eric.scala@free.fr
Crossing The River Styx *p89*
Little People Parliament
p220–221

MICHAEL SEE
http://michaelzhsee.cgsociety.
org/gallery
szxmiko02@yahoo.com
The Journey *p258*

GREG STAPLES
www.gregstaples.co.uk
gs@gregstaples.co.uk
© Wizards of the Coast
Serra Angel Vs Spectre
p306–307
© Wizards of the Coast
Solomon Cane *p18*
© Wandering Star/Davis Films
Productions
Zombie Psycho *p86–67*
© Wizards of the Coast

MIKE STAWICKI
www.mattstawicki.com
mstawicki@mattstawicki.com
The Fox *p320*

ANNE STOKES
www.annestokes.com
email@annestokes.com
Controller *p118*
Dragon Reflection *p8*, *p58*
Dragon's Nest *p298*
Scarlet Mage *p75*

J. P. TARGETE
www.targeteart.com
artmanagement@targeteart.
com
Arcana Evolved *p290–291*
Quag Keep *p31*

ROB THOMAS
www.mindsiphon.com
mindsiphon11@yahoo.com
Necro Warrior *p42*

FRANCIS TSAI
www.teamgt.com
tsai@teamgt.com
Magic Item *p48*
© Wizards of the Coast

LINDA TSO
www.epilogue.net/cgi/database/
art/list.pl?gallery=8270
lindatso@stickydoodle.com
Black Dandy *p174*
© Hotu Publishing

BORIS VALLEJO
www.imaginistix.com
The Junk Collector *p6*

CYRIL VAN DER HAEGEN
www.tegehel.org
tegehel@cox.net
Friday the 13th, October 1307
p300–301
The Last Tarot *p112*

ANTHONY S. WATERS
www.thinktankstudios.com
bightmei@thinktankstudios.
com
Awakening Maro *p194–195*
© Wizards of the Coast
Ravnica Forest *p284–285*
© Wizards of the Coast
Ravnica Mountains *p262–263*
© Wizards of the Coast
Ravnica Plains *p274–275*
© Wizards of the Coast

BENITA WINKLER
http://eeanee.com
benita@eeanee.com
Faydrums *p251*
Lovecats *p240*

KIEREN YANNER
www.kieranyanner.com
kieran@kieranyanner.com
Daniel *p239*
Death and the Serpent
of Caol *p217*

MICHAEL ZANCAN
http://zancan.fr
michael@zancan.fr
Backdoor to Luxuriance *p177*
Garden of Giants *p252*

Acknowledgments

A huge thank you to all the artists for their fantastic contributions, enthusiasm, and support.

Special thanks to:
Karen Hollingsworth,
Dave Morris, Lou Hankins,
Jim Pritchett, Lizzie Franke,
and most especially to
Mary McKenna.

▶ **The Fox**
Matt Stawicki
Book cover
The Fox from DAW
Adobe Photoshop and Corel Painter
www.mattstawicki.com

For his second book cover in this series, Matt found it interesting to return to a character for another portrayal: "The main character was much younger in the first book, and I'd relied on the environment to provide drama. However, with this piece I was able to really focus on the figure. The ship as the backdrop was a great element because of how off-kilter a boat can be. It's a great opportunity for a very dramatic angle."